Language: Usage and Practice, Grade 2

Contents

Contents continued

Contents continued

Unit 5: Capitalization and Punctuation

Unit 6: Composition

Language: Usage and Practice 2, SV 1419027794

INTRODUCTION

The *Language: Usage and Practice* series meets many needs.

- It is designed for students who require additional practice in the basics of effective writing and speaking.
- It provides focused practice in key grammar, usage, mechanics, and composition areas.
- It helps students gain ownership of essential skills.
- It presents practice exercises in a clear, concise format in a logical sequence.
- It allows for easy and independent use.

The *Language: Usage and Practice* lessons are organized into a series of units arranged in a logical sequence.

- vocabulary
- sentences
- grammar and usage
- mechanics of capitalization and punctuation
- composition skills

The *Language: Usage and Practice* lessons are carefully formatted for student comfort.

- Systematic, focused attention is given to just one carefully selected skill at a time.
- Rules are clearly stated at the beginning of each lesson and are illustrated with examples.
- Key terms are introduced in bold type.
- Meaningful practice exercises reinforce the skill.
- Each lesson is clearly labeled, and directions are clear and uncomplicated.

The *Language: Usage and Practice* series stresses the application of language principles in a variety of ways.

- Students are asked to match, circle, or underline elements in a predetermined sentence.
- Students are also asked to use what they have learned in an original sentence or in rewriting a sentence.

The *Language: Usage and Practice* series is designed for independent use.

- Because the format is logical and consistent and the vocabulary is carefully controlled, students can use *Language: Usage and Practice* with a high degree of independence.
- Copies of the worksheets can be given to individuals, pairs of students, or small groups for completion.
- Worksheets can be used in the language arts center.
- Worksheets can be given as homework for reviewing and reinforcing skills.

The *Language: Usage and Practice* series provides writing instruction.

- The process approach to teaching writing provides success for most students.
- *Language: Usage and Practice* provides direct support for the teaching of composition and significantly enhances those strategies and techniques commonly associated with the process-writing approach.
- Each book includes a composition unit that provides substantial work with composition skills, such as writing topic sentences, selecting supporting details, taking notes, writing reports, and revising and proofreading.
- Also included in the composition unit is practice with various prewriting activities, such as clustering and brainstorming, which play an important part in process writing.
- The composition lessons are presented in the same rule-plus-practice format as in the other units.

The *Language: Usage and Practice* series includes additional features.

- **Unit Tests**   Use the unit tests to check student progress and prepare students for standardized tests.
- **Sequential Support**   The content of each unit is repeated and expanded in subsequent levels as highlighted in the skills correlation chart on pages 5 and 6.
- **Assessment**   Use the Assessment on pages 7–10 to determine the skills your students need to practice.
- **Language Terms**   Provide each student with a copy of the list of language terms on page 120 to keep for reference throughout the year. Also place a copy in the classroom language arts center for reference.
- **Center Activities**   Use the worksheets as center activities to give students the opportunity to work cooperatively.

The *Language: Usage and Practice* series is a powerful tool!

**The activities use a variety of strategies to maintain student interest.
Watch your students' language improve as skills are
applied in structured, relevant practice!**

Skills Correlation

	1	2	3	4	5	6	7	8	High School
Vocabulary									
Rhyming Words	■	■							
Synonyms and Antonyms	■	■	■	■	■	■	■	■	■
Homonyms	■	■	■	■	■	■	■	■	■
Multiple Meanings/Homographs	■	■	■	■	■	■	■	■	■
Prefixes and Suffixes		■	■	■	■	■	■	■	■
Compound Words		■	■	■	■	■	■	■	■
Contractions		■	■	■	■	■	■	■	■
Idioms						■	■	■	■
Connotation/Denotation					■	■	■	■	
Sentences									
Word Order in Sentences	■	■		■					
Recognizing Sentences and Sentence Types	■	■	■	■	■	■	■	■	■
Subjects and Predicates	■	■	■	■	■	■	■	■	■
Compound/Complex Sentences			■	■	■	■	■	■	■
Sentence Combining		■	■	■	■	■	■	■	■
Run-on Sentences				■	■	■	■	■	■
Independent and Subordinate Clauses						■	■	■	■
Compound Subjects and Predicates	■			■	■	■	■	■	■
Direct and Indirect Objects					■		■	■	■
Inverted Word Order						■	■	■	■
Grammar and Usage									
Common and Proper Nouns	■	■	■	■	■	■	■	■	■
Singular and Plural Nouns	■	■	■	■	■	■	■	■	■
Possessive Nouns			■	■	■	■	■	■	■
Appositives						■	■	■	
Verbs and Verb Tense	■	■	■	■	■	■	■	■	■
Regular/Irregular Verbs	■	■	■	■	■	■	■	■	■
Subject/Verb Agreement	■	■	■	■	■	■	■	■	■
Verb Phrases						■	■	■	■
Transitive and Intransitive Verbs							■	■	
Verbals: Gerunds, Participles, and Infinitives							■	■	■
Active and Passive Voice							■	■	
Mood								■	
Pronouns	■	■	■	■	■	■	■	■	■
Antecedents					■		■	■	■
Articles	■	■	■		■	■			
Adjectives	■	■	■	■	■		■	■	■
Correct Word Usage (e.g., may/can, sit/set)	■		■	■	■	■	■	■	
Adverbs			■	■	■	■	■	■	
Prepositions						■	■	■	■
Prepositional Phrases						■	■	■	■
Conjunctions						■	■	■	■
Interjections						■	■		
Double Negatives								■	■
Capitalization and Punctuation									
Capitalization: First Word in Sentence	■	■	■	■	■	■	■	■	■
Capitalization: Proper Nouns	■	■	■	■	■	■	■	■	■
Capitalization: in Letters		■	■	■		■	■	■	■
Capitalization: Abbreviations and Titles		■	■	■	■	■	■	■	■
Capitalization: Proper Adjectives					■	■	■	■	■

Language: Usage and Practice 2, SV 1419027794

Capitalization and Punctuation (cont'd)	1	2	3	4	5	6	7	8	High School
End Punctuation	■	■	■	■	■	■	■	■	■
Commas		■	■	■	■	■	■	■	■
Apostrophes in Contractions		■	■	■	■	■	■	■	■
Apostrophes in Possessives			■	■	■	■	■	■	■
Quotation Marks			■	■	■	■	■	■	■
Colons/Semicolons					■	■	■	■	■
Hyphens						■	■	■	■
Composition									
Expanding Sentences			■		■	■	■	■	
Paragraphs: Topic Sentence (main idea)		■	■	■	■	■	■	■	■
Paragraphs: Supporting Details		■	■	■	■	■	■	■	■
Order in Paragraphs			■	■	■	■	■		■
Writing Process:									
Audience				■	■	■	■	■	
Topic			■	■	■	■	■	■	
Outlining				■		■	■	■	
Clustering/Brainstorming					■		■	■	
Note Taking						■			
Revising/Proofreading					■	■	■	■	
Types of Writing:									
Poem	■								
Letter	■	■	■			■			
"How-to" Paragraph			■						
Invitation			■						
Telephone Message			■						
Conversation				■					
Narrative Paragraph				■					
Comparing and Contrasting					■				
Descriptive Paragraph					■				
Report						■			
Interview							■		
Persuasive Composition								■	
Readiness/Study Skills									
Grouping	■		■						
Letters of Alphabet	■								
Listening	■	■							
Making Comparisons	■	■							
Organizing Information		■	■						
Following Directions	■	■	■	■	■				
Alphabetical Order	■	■	■	■	■				
Using a Dictionary:									
Definitions		■	■			■	■	■	
Guide Words/Entry Words		■	■	■	■	■	■	■	
Syllables and Pronunciation					■	■	■	■	
Multiple Meanings		■				■	■	■	
Word Origins						■	■		
Parts of a Book		■					■		
Using the Library						■	■	■	
Using Encyclopedias				■	■	■	■	■	
Using Reference Books						■	■	■	
Using the *Readers' Guide*							■	■	
Using Tables, Charts, Graphs, and Diagrams								■	
Choosing Appropriate Sources						■	■	■	

www.harcourtschoolsupply.com

Skills Correlation
Language: Usage and Practice 2, SV 1419027794

Name _____ Date _____

Assessment

 Look at the picture. Follow the directions.

1. Put an X on the apple.

2. Put an X to the right of the apple.

3. Put an X above the apple.

4. Draw a circle around the apple.

 Look at the map, and read the directions to Jesse's house. Then answer the questions.

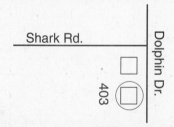 

1) Go east on Shark Road.

2) Turn south on Dolphin Drive.

3) Walk down two houses to 403 Dolphin Drive.

5. What direction should you go first? _____

6. What street should you walk on first? _____

7. Which direction should you turn? _____

8. What street should you turn on? _____

9. How many houses down Dolphin Drive is Jesse's house? _____

Language: Usage and Practice 2, SV 1419027794

Name _____ Date _____

 Cross out the word that does not belong.

10. cup   plate   fork   pen

11. boat   car   name   train

12. tree   door   flower   bush

 Write these words in alphabetical order.

13. Zena _____   14. door _____

　　Carol _____   　　window _____

　　Thomas _____   　　carpet _____

 Underline the words that would be on the same page as these guide words.

　　　　day / fish

15. dear   laugh   pig   knob

16. red   sell   egg   dark

17. bait   dust   gold   map

Use the dictionary words to answer the questions.

bill 1. a bird's beak	**boil** to heat a liquid until bubbles form
2. a paper that shows how much you owe	**box** a container used for storing things

18. Which word has two meanings? _____

19. Which word means "a container used for storing things"? _____

20. What does boil mean? _____

_____

Assessment
Language: Usage and Practice 2, SV 1419027794

Name _____ Date _____

 Read the words in the box. Then follow the directions.

narrow	pan	angry	short	knew	big

21. Write the words from the box that rhyme.

due _____ man _____

22. Write the words from the box that mean almost the same.

mad _____ large _____

23. Write the words from the box that mean the opposite.

tall _____ wide _____

 Circle the correct word to complete each sentence.

24. I went (to, too, two) the park.

25. I am going to (hear, here) the band today.

26. I will meet my friends (there, their).

 **Write T before the telling sentence. Write A before
the asking sentence. Write X before the group of
words that is not a sentence. Circle the naming parts.
Underline the action parts.**

_____ **27.** Who took my book?

_____ **28.** To get better.

_____ **29.** I bought some medicine.

 **Circle the special naming words. Underline the
action words.**

30. Mr. Donaldson grows his own vegetables.

31. He plants some of the vegetables in April.

Language: Usage and Practice 2, SV 1419027794

Name _____ Date _____

 Circle the word that best completes each sentence.

32. Rajib and I (was, were) out of town last week.

33. (We, They) went to Vancouver.

34. Rajib took (a, an) camera.

 Circle each letter that should be a capital letter. Write the correct punctuation marks for each sentence.

35. mr t r wiggins and i went to daytona beach last saturday sunday and monday

36. rhonda went to the beach last august

37. didnt she take her cat named whiskers

 Read the paragraph. Circle the main idea, and underline the supporting details.

38.   Julia wanted to bake her friend a cake for his birthday. First, Julia read the recipe. Then, she baked the cake. After the cake cooled, she put frosting on it.

 Write 1, 2, 3, or 4 to show what happened first, second, third, and last.

39.   Amy made her bed. First, she pulled up the top sheet. Next, she made the blanket even on all sides. Then, she shook the pillow. Last, she laid the quilt across the bed.

_____ Then, she shook the pillow.

_____ Next, she made the blanket even on all sides.

_____ Last, she laid the quilt across the bed.

_____ First, she pulled up the top sheet.

Language: Usage and Practice 2, SV 1419027794

Listening for Directions

- Always pay attention when you are listening for directions.
- Think about what the person is saying.
- Ask for the directions again if you did not hear or understand them.

 Look at the picture. Follow the directions given by your teacher.

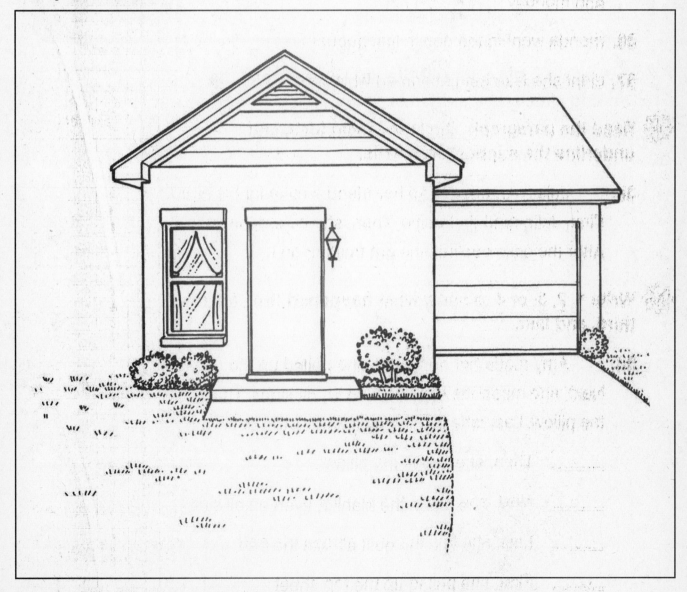

Teacher directions are in the answer key on page 121.

More Listening for Directions

- Listen carefully to all directions.
- Pay close attention to **key words**, or words that are important.
- Be sure you understand the order in which you are supposed to do things.

  EXAMPLE: You are planting some flowers. First, you prepare the soil. Then, you plant the seeds. Finally, you water the seeds.

  Key words numbered in order:
  1) prepare the soil
  2) plant the seeds
  3) water the seeds

 Listen to the directions. Write the key words in the order in which they should be done.

1. 1) _____

   2) _____

   3) _____

2. 1) _____

   2) _____

   3) _____

3. 1) _____

   2) _____

   3) _____

4. 1) _____

   2) _____

   3) _____

Teacher directions are in the answer key on page 121.

Unit 1: Study Skills
Language: Usage and Practice 2, SV 1419027794

Name _____ Date _____

Following Directions

 Read and follow the directions. Write the words that
are in the boxes.

---

1. Put an X [above] the doghouse.

_____

3. Put an X [under] the doghouse.

_____

---

2. Put an X [on] the doghouse.

_____

4. Put an X [inside] the doghouse.

_____

---

5. Put an X [beside] the doghouse on the [left].

_____ _____

---

6. Put an X [beside] the doghouse on the [right].

_____ _____

Following Written Directions

 Read the sentences. Follow the directions.

1. A fast horse runs down a wet street. Color the horse **brown**. Color the street **gray**. Color the water on the street **blue**.

2. A little car has a flat tire. Color the car **yellow**. Color the tires **black**.

3. Two boats go down a river. Color the boats **pink**. Color the sails **blue**.

4. A long flag hangs from a big balloon. Color the flag **red**. Color the balloon **purple**.

5. A big tent is beside four tall trees. Color the tent **orange**. Color the trees **green**.

6. An airplane flies in the sky. Color the airplane **gray**.

Name _____ Date _____

Following Directions to a Place

- **Directions** must be followed step-by-step.
- **Maps** can help you follow directions. They show you which way is north, south, east, and west by using the letters <u>N</u>, <u>S</u>, <u>E</u>, and <u>W</u>.

EXAMPLE:

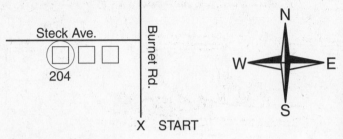

Directions to Shanell's House
   1) Go north on Burnet Road.
   2) Turn west on Steck Avenue.
   3) Walk down 3 houses to 204 Steck Avenue.

 Look at the map, and read the directions to Martin's house. Then answer the questions.

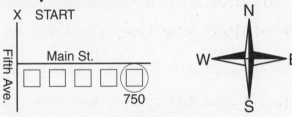

   1) Go south on Fifth Avenue.
   2) Turn east on Main Street.
   3) Walk down 5 houses to 750 Main Street.

1. What direction should you go first? _____

2. What street should you walk on first? _____

3. What direction should you go next? _____

4. What street should you be on? _____

5. How many houses down Main Street is Martin's house? _____

Language: Usage and Practice 2, SV 1419027794

Making Comparisons

 Look at the picture of Robert and Sara. Then answer the questions.

1. Who has the larger dog? _____

2. Who has the smaller dog? _____

3. Who has longer pants? _____

4. Who has shorter pants? _____

5. Who has shorter hair? _____

6. Who has longer hair? _____

7. Who has lighter hair? _____

8. Who has darker hair? _____

9. Who is shorter? _____

10. Who is taller? _____

www.harcourtschoolsupply.com
16
Unit 1: Study Skills
Language: Usage and Practice 2, SV 1419027794

Name _____ Date _____

Organizing Information

Cross out the word in each line that does not belong.
The first one is done for you.

1. red   blue   white   ~~turtle~~
2. jump   play   dog   run
3. elephant   Kim   Tony   Eva
4. book   frog   pencil   paper
5. cat   fish   raccoon   sister
6. happy   popcorn   sad   angry
7. breakfast   lunch   candle   supper
8. milk   water   juice   mud
9. cry   doll   ball   game
10. above   under   blue   beside

 Read the words in the box. Write each word in the correct group.

red	blue	write	green	sing	Vince
eat	dance	yellow	skip	Roberto	talk
Josh	Lupe	Mei	orange	Jennifer	pink

Colors	Names	Actions
red	Josh	eat

Unit 1: Study Skills
Language: Usage and Practice 2, SV 1419027794

Name _____ Date _____

Letters in ABC Order

 Write the missing letters.

A B C D _____

_____

_____

_____

 Write the letter that comes next.

1. S T __U__   5. M N _____   9. X Y _____

2. H I _____   6. K L _____   10. O P _____

3. B C _____   7. V W _____   11. D E _____

4. P Q _____   8. E F _____   12. J K _____

 Write the letter that comes in the middle.

13. J __K__ L   17. W _____ Y   21. S _____ U

14. E _____ G   18. C _____ E   22. A _____ C

15. Q _____ S   19. T _____ V   23. L _____ N

16. F _____ H   20. M _____ O   24. D _____ F

 Write the letter that comes before.

25. __A__ B C   29. _____ J K   33. _____ Q R

26. _____ T U   30. _____ F G   34. _____ S T

27. _____ N O   31. _____ L M   35. _____ V W

28. _____ X Y   32. _____ H I   36. _____ K L

Unit 1: Study Skills
Language: Usage and Practice 2, SV 1419027794

Name _____ Date _____

Words in ABC Order

 Number the words in ABC order. Then write the words
in the right order.

1.
2 bat   1. air
1 air   2. bat
3 cat   3. cat

6.
___ neck   1. _____
___ owl   2. _____
___ mail   3. _____

2.
___ top   1. _____
___ sea   2. _____
___ rock   3. _____

7.
___ well   1. _____
___ us   2. _____
___ very   3. _____

3.
___ egg   1. _____
___ fish   2. _____
___ dog   3. _____

8.
___ yes   1. _____
___ zoo   2. _____
___ X-ray   3. _____

4.
___ hat   1. _____
___ ice   2. _____
___ gate   3. _____

9.
___ pan   1. _____
___ oak   2. _____
___ nail   3. _____

5.
___ joke   1. _____
___ lake   2. _____
___ king   3. _____

10.
___ bat   1. _____
___ air   2. _____
___ cat   3. _____

Unit 1: Study Skills
Language: Usage and Practice 2, SV 1419027794

Finding Words in a Dictionary

- A **dictionary** is a book of words. The words in a dictionary are in ABC order.
- **Guide words** are at the top of every dictionary page. All the words on the page are in ABC order between these two words.
- The guide word on the left is the first word on the dictionary page.
- The guide word on the right is the last word on the dictionary page.

  EXAMPLE: **baby / bed**

  baby

  bed

 Use the dictionary page in the EXAMPLE above to answer these questions.

1. What is the first word on the above page? _____

2. What is the last word on the above page? _____

 Choose the pair of guide words below that you would use to find each word.

| fit / fun | race / run | see / sit |

3. sent ____ see / sit _____

4. flag _____

5. room _____

6. four _____

7. ranch _____

8. sheep _____

Language: Usage and Practice 2, SV 1419027794

Using a Dictionary

- A dictionary shows how to spell words.
- A dictionary tells what words mean.

---

many   a large number

middle   in between

neighbor   someone who lives in the next house

new   never used before

noise   a sound that is loud

open   not shut

paw   the foot of an animal

return   to go back

 Use the dictionary words to answer the questions.

1. What word means "in between"? _____

2. What word means "the foot of an animal"? _____

3. What word means "not shut"? _____

4. What word means "a sound that is loud"? _____

5. What word means "a large number"? _____

6. What word means "someone who lives in the next house"?

_____

7. What does <u>return</u> mean? _____

8. What does <u>new</u> mean? _____

21

Words in a Dictionary

> **always**   at all times
>
> **animal**   a living thing that is not a plant
>
> **bed**   a place to sleep
>
> **dark**   without light
>
> **green**   the color of grass
>
> **hay**   grass cut, and dried, and used as food
>   for cows and horses
>
> **hungry**   needing food
>
> **kitten**   a young cat
>
> **ladder**   a set of steps used to climb up and down
>
> **library**   a building where books are kept

 Use the dictionary words to answer the questions.
Write <u>yes</u> or <u>no</u> on the lines.

1. Is <u>hay</u> something that alligators eat? _____

2. Is the sunrise <u>always</u> in the morning? _____

3. Is a <u>bed</u> a place for swimming? _____

4. Is grass <u>green</u>? _____

5. Is a flower an <u>animal</u>? _____

6. Can you use a <u>ladder</u> to climb to the roof? _____

7. Is it <u>dark</u> outside at night? _____

8. Is a <u>library</u> a place for food? _____

9. Are you <u>hungry</u> after having lunch? _____

10. Is a baby pig called a <u>kitten</u>? _____

Name _____ Date _____

More Than One Meaning

- Some words have more than one meaning.
  EXAMPLE: **pet** 1. animal kept as a friend
                    2. to stroke
  Michelle has a **pet** turtle. (meaning 1)
  Casey loves to **pet** his new puppy.
  (meaning 2)

 Read the meanings. Circle the first meaning. Draw a line under the second meaning.

cold 1. not warm 2. a sickness of the
          nose and throat

tie 1. to fasten together with string
         2. a cloth worn around the neck

wave 1. moving water
          2. to move the hand back and forth
          as a greeting

 Choose the correct word from above to complete each sentence. Write the number of the dictionary meaning that goes with each sentence. The first is done for you.

1. Please _____tie_____ your shoelaces. __1__

2. Chris gave Dad a new _____ for his birthday. _____

3. Liv splashed in a big _____ at the beach. _____

4. I always _____ to my friends in school. _____

5. Put on a coat if you feel _____. _____

6. Del had a _____ and missed school today. _____

Language: Usage and Practice 2, SV 1419027794

Table of Contents

> • The **table of contents** is a list at the beginning of a book. It shows the titles and page numbers of what is in the book.

Table of Contents

 Use the Table of Contents to answer these questions.

1. What is this book about? _____

2. On what page can you read about cats? _____

3. On what page can you read about choosing a pet? _____

4. On what page can you read about exercising a pet? _____

5. What can you read about on page 24? _____

6. What can you read about on page 30? _____

7. How many kinds of pets can you read about? _____

8. On what page can you read about white mice? _____

9. What can you read about on page 17? _____

10. What can you read about on page 26? _____

Language: Usage and Practice 2, SV 1419027794

Unit 1 Test

Darken the circle by the apple with an <u>X</u> on it.

1. Ⓐ   Ⓑ   Ⓒ

Darken the circle by the train with an <u>X</u> beside it, on the right.

2. Ⓐ   Ⓑ   Ⓒ

Darken the circle by the butterfly with a circle around it.

3. Ⓐ    Ⓑ   Ⓒ

Look at the map, and read the directions. Then answer the questions. Darken the circle by the correct answer.

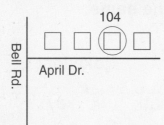

Directions to Roberto's House

1) Go south on Bell Road.
2) Turn east on April Drive.
3) Walk down three houses to 104 April Drive.

4. Which direction do you go first?

Ⓐ north   Ⓑ east   Ⓒ south

5. How many houses down April Drive is Roberto's house?

Ⓐ 4   Ⓑ 3   Ⓒ 2

Language: Usage and Practice 2, SV 1419027794

Name _____ Date _____

Darken the circle by the word that does not belong.

6. Ⓐ tree   Ⓑ flower   Ⓒ rug   10. Ⓐ boy   Ⓑ cake   Ⓒ man

7. Ⓐ milk   Ⓑ name   Ⓒ juice   11. Ⓐ pink   Ⓑ car   Ⓒ boat

8. Ⓐ cup   Ⓑ plate   Ⓒ open   12. Ⓐ red   Ⓑ blue   Ⓒ swim

9. Ⓐ ball   Ⓑ cat   Ⓒ dog   13. Ⓐ car   Ⓑ grass   Ⓒ truck

Darken the circle by the list that is in ABC order.

14. Ⓐ bird   Ⓑ dark   Ⓒ bird   16. Ⓐ nine   Ⓑ rest   Ⓒ mill
     dark   king   king   rest   mill   nine
     king   bird   dark   mill   nine   rest

15. Ⓐ map   Ⓑ zoo   Ⓒ cat   17. Ⓐ door   Ⓑ fun   Ⓒ door
     zoo   cat   map   knob   door   fun
     cat   map   zoo   fun   knob   knob

Darken the circle by the word that would be on the same page as the guide words.

         day/fish   **joke/lost**

18. Ⓐ dear   Ⓑ laugh   Ⓒ pig   21. Ⓐ park   Ⓑ key   Ⓒ snow

19. Ⓐ red   Ⓑ sell   Ⓒ egg   22. Ⓐ today   Ⓑ could   Ⓒ lamp

20. Ⓐ ball   Ⓑ dog   Ⓒ goat   23. Ⓐ jot   Ⓑ ice   Ⓒ meat

Darken the circle by the sentence that goes with definition #1.

24. Ⓐ I saw a bat at the zoo.

     Ⓑ Are you afraid of bats?

     Ⓒ Our team has a new bat.

     Ⓓ Bats can see at night.

> **bat**   **1.** a wooden stick used to play baseball
>   **2.** an animal that flies at night

Unit 1 Test
Language: Usage and Practice 2, SV 1419027794

Name _____ Date _____

Words That Rhyme

- Words that end with the same sound are called **rhyming words**.
  EXAMPLES: boy—toy   dog—log   cat—sat

 **Find a rhyming word on the ducks.
Write it on the line.**

dish
ring

door
ship

duck
hop

1. stop _____

3. floor _____

5. trip _____

2. sing _____

4. fish _____

6. truck _____

 **Finish each question. Use a rhyming word
from the tree.**

7. Did you ever see a goat
   wearing a _____?

8. Did you ever see a bug
   as big as a _____?

9. Did you ever see a bee
   get stuck in a _____

10. Did you ever see a fox
    carry a _____?

11. Did you ever see a duck
    driving a _____?

12. Did you ever see a pig
    wearing a _____?

box
coat
rug
tree
truck
wig

Language: Usage and Practice 2, SV 1419027794

Name _____ Date _____

Words That Mean the Same

- Words that mean almost the same thing are called **synonyms**.
  EXAMPLES:

grin—smile   sleep—rest

 Read each sentence below. Find a synonym in the box for each underlined word. Write it on the line.

dog	dad	gift	large	great	home
road	sad	sick	sleep	small	yell

1. I walked across the <u>street</u>. _____

2. I went into my <u>house</u>. _____

3. I was so <u>unhappy</u>. _____

4. I almost felt <u>ill</u>. _____

5. It was my birthday. No one gave me a <u>present</u>. _____

6. Then I saw something <u>little</u>. _____

7. It had <u>big</u> eyes. _____

8. It was a little <u>puppy</u>. _____

9. I began to <u>shout</u>. _____

10. "What a <u>wonderful</u> present!" _____

11. My <u>father</u> did remember my birthday. _____

12. I don't think I will <u>rest</u> tonight. _____

Language: Usage and Practice 2, SV 1419027794

Words That Mean the Opposite

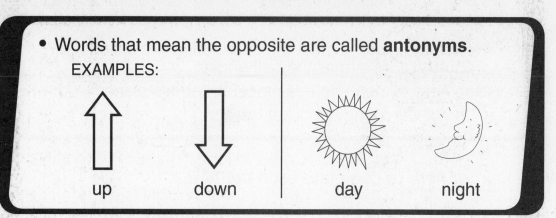

- Words that mean the opposite are called **antonyms**.
  EXAMPLES:

  up   down | day   night

 Draw a line to the antonym for each underlined word.

1. a <u>hard</u> bed   dark

2. a <u>short</u> story   happy

3. a <u>light</u> color   long

4. <u>off</u> the table   low

5. a <u>sad</u> movie   on

6. a <u>high</u> bridge   soft

 Write the antonym for the underlined word.

7. When you are not <u>wet</u>, you are _____. (happy, dry)

8. I like to run <u>fast</u>, not _____. (slow, far)

9. When food isn't <u>good</u>, it tastes _____. (hot, bad)

10. Summer is <u>hot</u>, and winter is _____. (cold, snow)

11. A traffic light turns red for <u>stop</u> and green for _____. (high, go)

12. Some questions are <u>easy</u>. Others are _____. (not, hard)

13. My shoes were <u>clean</u>. Then they got _____. (dirty, old)

14. The teacher will answer <u>yes</u> or _____. (maybe, no)

Words That Sound the Same

> • Use <u>hear</u> to mean "to listen to."
>   EXAMPLE: We **hear** the bell ringing.
> • Use <u>here</u> to mean "to this place" or "at this place."
>   EXAMPLE: Bring the ticket **here**.

✳ Write <u>hear</u> or <u>here</u> to complete each sentence.

1. Did you _____ that the circus is coming?

2. Is it coming _____ soon?

3. Yes, it will be _____ today.

4. I think I _____ the music now.

5. The parade is almost _____.

6. Come over _____ and watch it with me.

> • Use <u>their</u> to mean "something owned by two or
>   more people."
>   EXAMPLE: The children played with **their** balloons.
> • Use <u>there</u> to mean "in that place."
>   EXAMPLE: The circus tent is over **there**.

✳ Write <u>their</u> or <u>there</u> to complete each sentence.

7. The people showed _____ circus tickets.

8. And _____ seats were up high.

9. We put our coats _____ on the seats.

10. Some clowns did _____ tricks for us.

11. Did you see the elephants _____?

Language: Usage and Practice 2, SV 1419027794

They're Tearing Their Chair There

- Use <u>there</u> when you mean "in that place."
  EXAMPLE: The dinosaur is over **there**.
- Use <u>their</u> when you mean "belonging to them."
  EXAMPLE: This is **their** swamp.
- <u>They're</u> is a contraction for "they are." Use <u>they're</u> when you mean "they are."
  EXAMPLE: **They're** eating leaves from the trees.

 Circle the correct word in ( ) to complete each sentence.

1. Is this (their, they're) food?

2. (There, They're) huge animals.

3. A big one is over (there, their).

4. Once it was (there, their) land.

5. Dinosaurs lived (they're, there) for a while.

6. (They're, There) everywhere!

7. (They're, There) the two biggest dinosaurs.

8. The faster dinosaur is resting (their, there).

9. Small dinosaurs lived (they're, there) long ago.

10. (Their, There) land was different then.

11. I see some more dinosaurs over (they're, there).

12. (They're, There) in the lake.

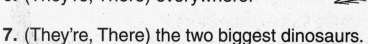

More Words That Sound the Same

> • Use <u>write</u> to mean "to put words on paper."
>   EXAMPLE: Please **write** your name on your paper.
> • Use <u>right</u> to mean "correct."
>   EXAMPLE: Your answer is **right**.
> • Use <u>right</u> to mean "the opposite of left."
>   EXAMPLE: Turn **right** to get to my school.

Write <u>right</u> or <u>write</u> to complete each sentence.

1. Chris likes to _____ on the board.

2. Everything was _____ on Marta's math paper.

3. We turn _____ to go to the lunchroom.

4. Our class is learning to _____ stories.

5. Kim drew the picture on the _____ side.

6. Did you _____ a letter to your grandma?

7. Luisa can _____ in Spanish.

8. The teacher marked the _____ answers.

9. Be sure you do the _____ page.

10. Jenna will _____ about her birthday party.

11. Jim colors with his _____ hand.

 Write two sentences about school. Use <u>write</u> in one sentence. Use <u>right</u> in the other sentence.

12. _____

13. _____

Other Words That Sound the Same

- Use <u>two</u> to mean "the number 2."
  EXAMPLE: **Two** children worked together.
- Use <u>too</u> to mean "more than enough."
  EXAMPLE: There are **too** many people on the bus.
- Use <u>too</u> to mean "also."
  EXAMPLE: May I help, **too**?
- Use <u>to</u> to mean "toward" or "to do something."
  EXAMPLE: Let's go **to** the library **to** find Kim.

 Write two, too, or to to complete each sentence.

1. The children were working _____ make a class library.

2. Andrew had _____ books in his hand.

3. He gave them _____ Ms. Diaz.

4. Ms. Diaz was happy _____ get the books.

5. "We can never have _____ many books," she said.

6. Rosa said she would bring _____ or three books.

7. Deon wanted to bring some, _____ .

8. Britney found a book that was _____ old.

9. Pages started _____ fall out when she picked it up.

10. The bookcase was almost _____ small.

11. Soon everyone would have new books _____ read.

12. We can take out _____ of these books at a time.

13. "Others can enjoy our books, _____ ," said Chang.

14. Books can be good friends _____ us.

Unit 2: Vocabulary
Language: Usage and Practice 2, SV 1419027794

Words That Have Two Meanings

 Look at each pair of pictures. Read each sentence. Then write the letter of the correct meaning on the line.

bat

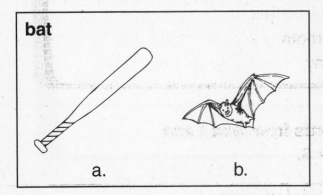

a.   b.

1. _____ Tony has a wooden bat.

2. _____ The bat sleeps during the day.

3. _____ The bat broke when Alberto hit the ball.

pitcher

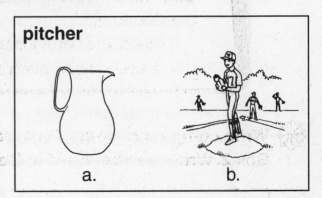

a.   b.

7. _____ The pitcher threw the ball too low.

8. _____ I put some juice in the pitcher.

9. _____ The pitcher of milk was empty.

plant

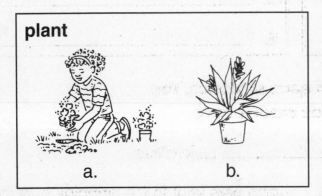

a.   b.

4. _____ Kendra wants to plant a tree.

5. _____ The farmer will plant his crops in the fall.

6. _____ Jody grew a plant at school.

light

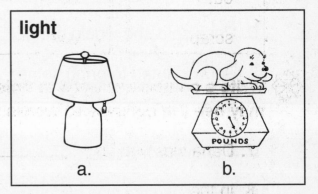

a.   b.

10. _____ I will turn on the light.

11. _____ The puppy is light.

12. _____ There is only one light in my room.

Language: Usage and Practice 2, SV 1419027794

Name _____ Date _____

Compound Words

> • Sometimes two words can be put together to make a new word. The new word is called a **compound word**.
>   EXAMPLES:
>   lunch + room = lunchroom
>   every + day = everyday

 Write compound words. Pick words from Box 1 and Box 2. Write the new word in Box 3.

Box 1	Box 2	Box 3
sun	noon	1. _____
after	glasses	2. _____
play	side	3. _____
birth	ground	4. _____
out	book	5. _____
scrap	day	6. _____

 Write a compound word to finish each sentence. You may use the compound words you made above.

7. Dana was wearing _____ in class.

8. In the _____, Dana was sent to the principal's office.

9. Amy put a picture of the school in her _____.

10. Brad will be eight years old on his next _____.

11. We can't go _____ if it rains.

12. The _____ will be too wet.

Language: Usage and Practice 2, SV 1419027794

Prefixes

- A **prefix** is a group of letters added to the beginning of a word.
- Adding a prefix to a word changes its meaning.
  EXAMPLES:
      The old woman was <u>happy</u>.
      The old woman was <u>unhappy</u>.

Prefix	Meaning	Example
un	not	<u>un</u>clear
re	again	<u>re</u>write

 Read each sentence. Underline the word that has a prefix. Tell the meaning of the word.

1. The old man was unable to find something to wear.

_____

2. The old woman reopened the drawer.

_____

3. She told the old man they were unlucky.

_____

4. The old man felt this was unfair.

_____

5. He was very unhappy.

_____

6. The woman asked the man to rewind the yarn.

_____

7. The old woman rewashed the socks.

_____

8. Could the socks be uneven?

_____

9. The old man refilled his wife's glass.

_____

10. The farmer's wife reknitted the sweater.

_____

Name _____ Date _____

Suffixes

- A **suffix** is a group of letters added to the end of a word.
- Adding a suffix to a word changes its meaning.
  EXAMPLES:
  Adam's parents were <u>helpless</u>.
  The doctor was <u>helpful</u>.

Suffix	Meaning	Example
ful	full of	hope<u>ful</u>
less	without	use<u>less</u>
able	able to be	break<u>able</u>

 Read each sentence. Underline the word that has a suffix. Tell the meaning of the word.

1. Is Jena careful? _____

2. Paul thought the game was harmless. _____

3. The chair Alli was on was breakable. _____

 Complete each sentence with a word from the box. Tell the meaning of the word you chose.

    hopeful   dreadful   thankful

4. Alli's parents had a _____ shock!

_____

5. They were _____ the chair would not break.

_____

6. When Dean came out of the hospital, he was very _____.

_____

Unit 2 Test

Darken the circle by the correct word that completes each sentence.

1. A word that rhymes with <u>bake</u> is ___.

   Ⓐ take   Ⓑ goat   Ⓒ cook

2. A word that rhymes with <u>ship</u> is ___.

   Ⓐ boat   Ⓑ drip   Ⓒ shut

3. <u>Grin</u> means almost the same as ___.

   Ⓐ pin   Ⓑ cry   Ⓒ smile

4. <u>House</u> means almost the same as ___.

   Ⓐ trip   Ⓑ home   Ⓒ mouse

5. The opposite of <u>long</u> is ___.

   Ⓐ song   Ⓑ tall   Ⓒ short

6. The opposite of <u>hot</u> is ___.

   Ⓐ cold   Ⓑ warm   Ⓒ pot

7. Did you ___ about the prize?

   Ⓐ hear   Ⓑ here   Ⓒ there

8. Jenna and Chris will bring ___ books to the library.

   Ⓐ there   Ⓑ their   Ⓒ hear

9. I have learned how to ___ all the spelling words.

   Ⓐ right   Ⓑ wrote   Ⓒ write

10. Our class wants ___ play outside today.

    Ⓐ to   Ⓑ too   Ⓒ two

11. I have ___ many books to carry!

    Ⓐ to   Ⓑ too   Ⓒ two

Language: Usage and Practice 2, SV 1419027794

Name _____ Date _____

Darken the circle by the correct word that completes each sentence.

12. ___ is a compound word.
  Ⓐ office   Ⓑ meaning   Ⓒ birthday

13. The word with a prefix is ___.
  Ⓐ apple   Ⓑ unhappy   Ⓒ real

14. The word with a prefix is ___.
  Ⓐ refill   Ⓑ hopeful   Ⓒ notebook

15. The word with a suffix is ___.
  Ⓐ lunchroom   Ⓑ unfair   Ⓒ harmless

16. The word with a suffix is ___.
  Ⓐ playground   Ⓑ useful   Ⓒ unclear

Look at each pair of pictures. Read each sentence. Then choose the letter of the correct meaning for the underlined word.

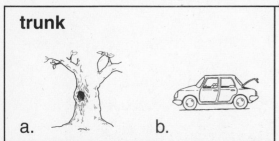

17. There was a large hole in the <u>trunk</u> of the tree.
  Ⓐ meaning <u>a</u>   Ⓑ meaning <u>b</u>

18. The spare tire for the car is in the <u>trunk</u>.
  Ⓐ meaning <u>a</u>   Ⓑ meaning <u>b</u>

19. Geese usually <u>fly</u> south for the winter.
  Ⓐ meaning <u>a</u>   Ⓑ meaning <u>b</u>

20. The <u>fly</u> kept buzzing in my ear.
  Ⓐ meaning <u>a</u>   Ⓑ meaning <u>b</u>

Name _____ Date _____

Sentences

> • A **sentence** is a group of words that tells or asks
> something. It stands for a complete thought.
>   EXAMPLES: Friends play. Do you play?

 **Write yes if the group of words is a sentence. Write no
if the group of words is not a sentence.**

1. ___no___ A long time ago.

2. _____ The class went to the park.

3. _____ Near the tree.

4. _____ Ten children played.

5. _____ Mark hit the ball.

6. _____ A dog chased the ball.

7. _____ Brad and Carlos.

8. _____ Ran and played all day.

9. _____ Did you have fun?

10. _____ Jan lost a new red shoe.

11. _____ We ate lunch.

12. _____ Too hot for us.

13. _____ The boys and girls talked.

14. _____ Some people.

15. _____ Sang songs.

16. _____ Will you go back to the park?

Language: Usage and Practice 2, SV 1419027794

Name _____ Date _____

More Sentences

 Draw lines between the groups of words to make sentences. Then read the sentences.

1. Mrs. Brown   live in our building.

2. Our building   is made of wood.

3. Four families   lives on my street.

4. The students   was climbing the tree.

5. Jennifer   went on a picnic.

6. The sun   shone all day.

7. Corn and beans   fed the baby goat.

8. The wagon   has a broken wheel.

9. The mother goat   grow on a farm.

10. The boat   sailed in strong winds.

11. The fisher   were sold in the store.

12. Some of the fish   caught seven fish.

13. Our team   hit the ball a lot.

14. Our batters   won ten games.

15. The ballpark   was full of fans.

 Write a sentence about your birthday.

_____

_____

 Write a sentence about your house or apartment.

_____

_____

Word Order in Sentences

- Words in a sentence must be in an order that makes sense.
  EXAMPLE: Grandpa plays baseball.

 **Write these words in an order that makes sense.
The first one is done for you.**

1. brother My apples eats

My brother eats apples
_____.

2. drinks Bo milk

_____.

3. butter peanut Kiyo likes

_____.

4. Justin bread wants

_____.

5. corn plants Arturo

_____.

6. a fish Chang caught

_____.

7. breakfast cooks Dad

_____.

8. his shares Shawn lunch

_____.

9. the Rosa grew carrot

_____.

10. the looks at Katie pie

_____.

Name _____ Date _____

Telling Sentences

> • A **telling sentence** is a group of words that tells something.
>
> EXAMPLES: I feed my pony.
>
> Ponies like to run and play.

 Write telling on the line before the group of words if it is a telling sentence. Leave the line blank if it is not a sentence. The first one is done for you.

<u>telling</u>

1. Pat loves her pony.

_____ 2. His name is Zip.

_____ 3. Fast horses.

_____ 4. Zip can run fast.

_____ 5. He eats apples.

_____ 6. Over the hill.

_____ 7. Zip runs to Pat.

_____ 8. Zip has a long tail.

_____ 9. Pat and her mother.

_____ 10. His hair is soft.

_____ 11. After school.

_____ 12. Pat likes to play with Zip.

_____ 13. In the barn.

_____ 14. Pat brushes Zip.

_____ 15. You can ride Zip, too.

Language: Usage and Practice 2, SV 1419027794

Name _____ Date _____

Asking Sentences

> • An **asking sentence** is a group of words that asks a
> question. You can answer an asking sentence.
> EXAMPLES: How old are you?
> Where do you live?

✳ **Write <u>asking</u> on the line before the group of words if
it is an asking sentence. Leave the line blank if the
group of words is not a sentence.**

<u>   asking   </u>   **1.** Is this your friend?

_____ **2.** Where does she live?

_____ **3.** She in town?

_____ **4.** How was school today?

_____ **5.** Music and art?

_____ **6.** Do you want a snack?

_____ **7.** Where are the apples?

_____ **8.** Look in the?

_____ **9.** When does school begin?

_____ **10.** Do you have any brothers?

_____ **11.** Where can we work?

_____ **12.** The kitchen in?

_____ **13.** Can you ride a bike?

_____ **14.** Yes, I?

_____ **15.** Why did Sara cry?

Language: Usage and Practice 2, SV 1419027794

Kinds of Sentences

- A telling sentence is also called a **statement**. A statement is a sentence that tells something. It begins with a capital letter. It ends with a period (.).
  EXAMPLE: Jake gives some seeds to Kara.
- An asking sentence is also called a **question**. A question is a sentence that asks something. It begins with a capital letter. It ends with a question mark (?).
  EXAMPLE: Will Kara plant seeds?
- An **exclamation** is a sentence that shows strong feelings. It begins with a capital letter. It ends with an exclamation point (!).
  EXAMPLE: What a fine garden Jake has!

Read the sentences. Write statement for a telling sentence. Write question for an asking sentence. Write exclamation for a sentence that shows strong feelings.

_____ **1.** Jake was in his garden.

_____ **2.** Who came walking by?

_____ **3.** Kara stopped to look at the garden.

_____ **4.** What did Kara do?

_____ **5.** Kara read a story to her seeds.

_____ **6.** The seeds started to grow.

_____ **7.** What makes seeds grow?

_____ **8.** Kara works so hard!

_____ **9.** Her garden is big!

_____ **10.** It makes her happy.

Language: Usage and Practice 2, SV 1419027794

Name _____ Date _____

Making Kinds of Sentences

- Use a statement to tell something. End a statement with a period.
- Use a question to ask something. End a question with a question mark.
- Use an exclamation to show strong feelings. End an exclamation with an exclamation point.

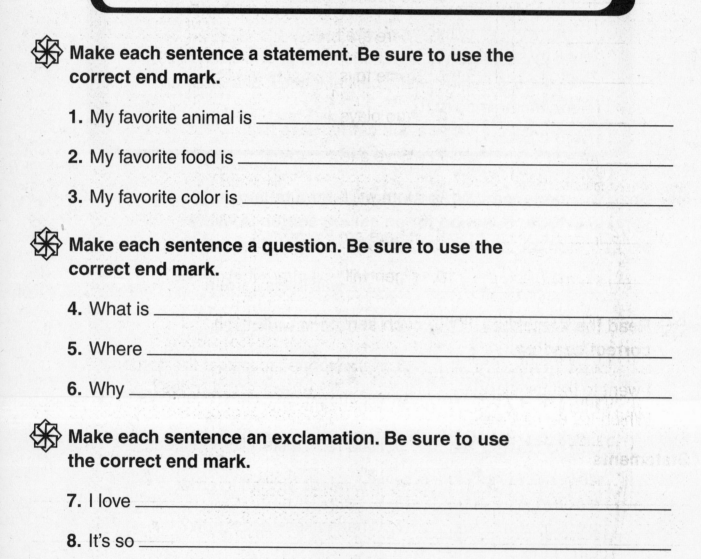

✿ **Make each sentence a statement. Be sure to use the correct end mark.**

1. My favorite animal is _____

2. My favorite food is _____

3. My favorite color is _____

✿ **Make each sentence a question. Be sure to use the correct end mark.**

4. What is _____

5. Where _____

6. Why _____

✿ **Make each sentence an exclamation. Be sure to use the correct end mark.**

7. I love _____

8. It's so _____

What Kind of Sentence Is It?

 Write **statement** for telling sentences. Write **question** for asking sentences.

_____ 1. Where is the toy store?

_____ 2. The toy store is near school.

_____ 3. Do you like kites?

_____ 4. There are balloons and balls.

_____ 5. Some toys can play music.

_____ 6. Who plays with markers?

_____ 7. I have a few games.

_____ 8. Mom will buy a puzzle.

_____ 9. Where are the bikes?

_____ 10. When will you play with bubbles?

Read the sentences. Write each sentence under the correct heading.

I went to the toy store.   Are there any puzzles?

Which toy do you want?   I picked a game.

Statements

_____

_____

Questions

_____

_____

Name _____ Date _____

Sentence Parts

- Every sentence has two parts.
- The **naming part** tells who or what the sentence is about. The naming part is called the **subject**.
- The **action part** tells something about the naming part. The action part is called the **predicate**.
- A naming part and an action part make a complete thought.

    EXAMPLE:

Naming Part	Action Part
Kara	plants some seeds.

 Each group of words needs a naming part or an action part. Add words to make each group of words a complete sentence.

1. Jake _____.

2. Kara _____.

3. _____ need sunshine and rain.

4. The flower seeds _____.

5. Jake and Kara _____.

6. _____ looks at the flower.

7. _____ grow in the garden.

8. The flowers _____.

9. _____ bloom in the spring.

10. _____ are my favorite flowers.

11. The butterflies _____.

12. _____ makes the flowers grow.

Language: Usage and Practice 2, SV 1419027794

Name _____   Date _____

Naming Part of Sentences

- The naming part of a sentence tells who or what the sentence is about.
  EXAMPLES: **Three mice** run away.
  The cat plays with a ball.

 Circle the naming part of each sentence. The first one is done for you.

1. (My family and I) live on a busy street.

2. Sandy Harper found a bird.

3. Miss Jenkins drives very slowly.

4. Mr. Olson walks his dog.

5. Levon throws to his dog.

6. Mr. Byrne cuts his grass.

7. Mrs. Osawa picks up her children.

8. Mr. and Mrs. Diaz shop for food.

9. Jeanie plays in the park.

10. Mr. Wolf brings the mail.

11. Tom Taft brings the paper.

12. Mr. O'Dowd cooks dinner.

13. Matt paints the house.

14. Some children plant a garden.

15. Mrs. Clark washes her windows.

16. Carolyn and Alberto plant flower seeds.

Language: Usage and Practice 2, SV 1419027794

Action Part of Sentences

> • The action part of a sentence tells what someone or something does.
>   EXAMPLES: Three mice **run away**.
>   The cat **plays with a ball**.

 Circle the action part of each sentence.

1. My family and I live on a busy street.

2. Sandy Harper found a bird.

3. Miss Jenkins drives very slowly.

4. Mr. Olson walks his dog.

5. Levon throws to his dog.

6. Mr. Byrne cuts his grass.

7. Mrs. Osawa picks up her children.

8. Mr. and Mrs. Diaz shop for food.

9. Jeanie plays in the park.

10. Mr. Wolf brings the mail.

11. Tom Taft brings the paper.

12. Mr. O'Dowd cooks dinner.

13. Matt paints the house.

14. Some children plant a garden.

15. Mrs. Clark washes her windows.

16. Carolyn and Alberto plant flower seeds.

Name _____ Date _____

Sentence Parts

 Choose a naming part from the box to complete each sentence.

Lions	Birds	A pig	A cat	My dog	Zebras	Fish

1. _____ roar loudly in their cages.

2. _____ have black and white stripes.

3. _____ rolls in the mud.

4. _____ plays with a ball of yarn.

5. _____ chews his new bone.

6. _____ swim in water.

7. _____ fly in the sky.

 Choose an action part from the box to complete each sentence.

barks	buzz	fly	hops	moo	quack	roar

8. Robins and blackbirds _____.

9. Yellow bees _____.

10. My little dog _____.

11. Mother Duck and her babies _____.

12. A rabbit with big feet _____.

13. Angry lions _____.

14. All the cows on the farm _____.

 Write a sentence about an animal that you like.
Circle the naming part. Underline the action part.

_____

_____

Language: Usage and Practice 2, SV 1419027794

Writing Clear Sentences

- A good writer uses exact **verbs**. Exact verbs give a clear picture of an action.

    EXAMPLE:

    Spaceships go to the moon. (Go is a weak verb in this sentence.)

    Spaceships zoom to the moon. (Zoom is an exact verb in this sentence.)

    How to Use Exact Verbs in Sentences:

    1. Picture the action. Think about what a person or thing is doing.
    2. Choose an action verb that tells exactly what the person or thing is doing.
    3. Use the action verb in a sentence.

 Think of a more exact verb for each underlined verb. Write the new word on the line.

1. People <u>walk</u> to work. _____

2. Trains <u>move</u> along the tracks. _____

3. We <u>ride</u> our bicycles. _____

4. Fast cars <u>go</u> up the road. _____

5. The airplane <u>flies</u> in the sky. _____

6. A man <u>runs</u> around the park. _____

7. The children <u>walk</u> to school. _____

8. A bus <u>goes</u> down the highway. _____

9. The boat <u>moves</u> near the shore. _____

10. The woman <u>says</u> the warning. _____

Language: Usage and Practice 2, SV 1419027794

Adding Describing Words to Sentences

- A good writer adds describing words to sentences to give a clear picture.

  EXAMPLE:

  The moth sat on top of a clover.

  The <u>black</u> moth sat on top of a <u>white</u> clover.

  (Colorful words added)

  How to Add Describing Words to Sentences:

  1. Look for sentences that do not give your reader a clear picture.
  2. Think of describing words that tell more about what things look like.
  3. Add the describing words to the sentences.

 **Add describing words to these sentences.
Write the new sentences.**

1. The clown wears a hat.

   _____

2. A lion jumps through a hoop.

   _____

3. A monkey rides on an elephant.

   _____

4. A butterfly flew into the tent.

   _____

www.harcourtschoolsupply.com
53
Unit 3: Sentences
Language: Usage and Practice 2, SV 1419027794

Beginning Sentences in Different Ways

- A good writer should not begin every sentence with the same noun.
- Sometimes the words <u>he</u>, <u>she</u>, <u>I</u>, <u>we</u>, and <u>they</u> are used in place of nouns.

EXAMPLE:

Ant climbed down a branch.
Ant was thirsty. <u>She</u> tried to get a drink.

How to Begin Sentences in Different Ways:

1. Look for sentences that begin with the same noun.
2. Use the word <u>he</u>, <u>she</u>, <u>I</u>, <u>we</u>, or <u>they</u> in place of the noun.
3. Write the new sentence.

✾ **Change the way some of these sentences begin.**
Begin some of them with <u>He</u>, <u>She</u>, <u>I</u>, <u>We</u> or <u>They</u>.
Write the new sentences.

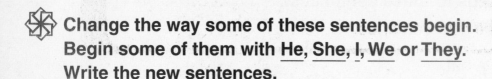

1. The ant climbed down a blade of grass. The ant fell into the spring.

_____

2. The bird pulled off a leaf. The bird let the leaf fall into the water.

_____

3. The hunter saw a lion. The hunter spread a net.

_____

4. The lion and I live in the woods. The lion and I are friends.

_____

Joining Sentences

- A good writer can join two short sentences. This makes the sentences more interesting to read.
- The word <u>and</u> is used to join the sentences.
- Sometimes the naming parts of two sentences are the same. The action parts can be joined.

  EXAMPLE:

  Jake planted seeds. Jake worked in his garden.

  Jake planted seeds <u>and</u> worked in his garden.

How to Join Sentences:

1. Look for sentences that have the same naming part.
2. Write the naming part.
3. Look for different action parts. Use the word <u>and</u> to join them.
4. Write the new sentence.

Use the word <u>and</u> to join each pair of sentences. Write the new sentences.

1. Jake gave seeds to Kara. Jake told her to plant them.

   _____

2. Kara planted the seeds. Kara looked at the ground.

   _____

3. Kara sang songs to her seeds. Kara read stories to them.

   _____

4. The rain fell on the seeds. The rain helped them grow.

   _____

Language: Usage and Practice 2, SV 1419027794

More Joining Sentences

- A good writer can join two short sentences. This makes the sentences more interesting to read.
- The word <u>and</u> is used to join the sentences.
- Sometimes the action parts of two sentences are the same. Then, the naming parts can be joined.

  EXAMPLE:

  The hunter stopped at the house. The bear stopped at the house.

  The hunter <u>and</u> the bear stopped at the house.

  How to Join Sentences:

  1. Look for sentences that have the same action part.
  2. Join the naming parts. Use the word <u>and</u>.
  3. Add the action part.

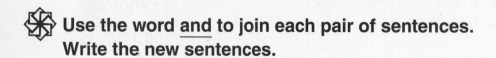 **Use the word <u>and</u> to join each pair of sentences. Write the new sentences.**

1. The farmer stood in the doorway. His family stood in the doorway.

   _____

2. The hunter stayed with the family. The bear stayed with the family.

   _____

3. The mice ran out the door. The children ran out the door.

   _____

4. The hunter went home. The bear went home.

   _____

Language: Usage and Practice 2, SV 1419027794

Unit 3 Test

Choose whether the group of words is a sentence. Darken the circle by <u>yes</u> or <u>no</u>.

1. Seven children from my class. Ⓐ yes   Ⓑ no

2. Joe and Marta are best friends. Ⓐ yes   Ⓑ no

3. Got here today. Ⓐ yes   Ⓑ no

4. Gina studied for the test. Ⓐ yes   Ⓑ no

5. Kathy doesn't know if. Ⓐ yes   Ⓑ no

6. Uncle Jeremy is out of town. Ⓐ yes   Ⓑ no

Darken the circle by the sentence in each group that is in an order that makes sense.

7. Ⓐ It time what is?
   Ⓑ What time is it?
   Ⓒ Time what it is?

8. Ⓐ Is caught my kite in a tree.
   Ⓑ Tree is a my kite caught is.
   Ⓒ My kite is caught in a tree.

9. Ⓐ My birthday is tomorrow.
   Ⓑ Tomorrow my birthday is.
   Ⓒ My is tomorrow birthday.

10. Ⓐ Circus the is fun.
    Ⓑ The circus is fun.
    Ⓒ Fun the circus is.

Darken the circle by <u>telling</u> or <u>asking</u> for each sentence.

11. Daisy is my dog. Ⓐ telling   Ⓑ asking

12. She can follow directions. Ⓐ telling   Ⓑ asking

13. Does she have a doghouse? Ⓐ telling   Ⓑ asking

14. She stays in our house. Ⓐ telling   Ⓑ asking

15. Where does Daisy play? Ⓐ telling   Ⓑ asking

  Language: Usage and Practice 2, SV 1419027794

Name _____ Date _____

Darken the circle by naming part or action part to tell about the underlined words in each sentence.

16. Megan studied for her test.   Ⓐ naming part   Ⓑ action part

17. The children on my street play together.   Ⓐ naming part   Ⓑ action part

18. My little sister loves to play soccer.   Ⓐ naming part   Ⓑ action part

19. I will go to school.   Ⓐ naming part   Ⓑ action part

20. My brother loves to swim.   Ⓐ naming part   Ⓑ action part

21. Janet's grandparents went to the coast.   Ⓐ naming part   Ⓑ action part

22. The winner gets a blue ribbon.   Ⓐ naming part   Ⓑ action part

23. A farmer plants crops.   Ⓐ naming part   Ⓑ action part

Add descriptive words to make the sentence more interesting. Write the new sentence.

24. The children ran through the woods.

_____

Change the way the sentence begins. Use He, She, I, We, or They. Write the new sentence.

25. My mother packed a lunch for the picnic.

_____

Use the word and to join each pair of sentences. Write the new sentences.

26. Ava went to the movie. Alex went to the movie.

_____

27. Chad mowed the lawn. Chad raked the leaves.

_____

Naming Words

- A **noun** is a word that names a person, place, or thing. The words <u>a</u>, <u>an</u>, and <u>the</u> are clues that show a noun is near.

    EXAMPLES: a **man**, the **yard**, an **elephant**

 Find the nouns, or naming words, below. Write the nouns on the lines. The first one has been done for you.

apple	car	eat	hear	rug
bird	chair	girl	hot	tree
boy	desk	gone	over	truck
came	dirty	grass	pen	up

1. _apple_   5. _____   9. _____

2. _____   6. _____   10. _____

3. _____   7. _____   11. _____

4. _____   8. _____   12. _____

 Draw lines under the two nouns in each sentence. Then write the nouns on the lines.

13. The girl eats an apple.   _____ _____

14. A bird flies to the tree.   _____ _____

15. A chair is by the desk.   _____ _____

16. A boy sits in the chair.   _____ _____

17. The girl plays with a truck.   _____ _____

18. The truck is on the rug.   _____ _____

Language: Usage and Practice 2, SV 1419027794

Name _____   Date _____

Special Naming Words

> - A noun is a word that names a person, place, or thing.
> - A **proper noun** is a word that names a special person, place, or thing.
> - A proper noun begins with a capital letter.
>
> | EXAMPLES: | **Noun** | **Proper Noun** |
> |---|---|---|
> | | girl | Karen Stone |
> | | park | City Park |
> | | bread | Tasty Bread |

 Find the proper nouns in the box below. Write the proper nouns on the lines. The first one is done for you.

baseball	China	prince	man
Bob's Bikes	Elf Corn	New York City	robin
Bridge Road	Gabe	Ohio	State Street
children	Linda	Pat Green	town

1. __Bob's Bikes__   6. _____

2. _____   7. _____

3. _____   8. _____

4. _____   9. _____

5. _____   10. _____

 Draw a line under the proper noun in each sentence. Then write the proper noun on the line.

11. I bought apples at Hill's Store. _____

12. The store is on Baker Street. _____

13. It is near Stone Library. _____

14. I gave an apple to Emily Fuller. _____

Language: Usage and Practice 2, SV 1419027794

Name _____ Date _____

Singular and Plural Nouns

- A **singular noun** names one person, place, or thing.
- A **plural noun** names more than one person, place, or thing.
- Add <u>s</u> to most nouns to make them mean "more than one."
    EXAMPLES: One <u>girl</u> wears a black hat.
    Many <u>girls</u> wear funny masks.

 Circle the correct noun to complete each sentence.

1. Two (boy, boys) went out on Halloween.

2. A (girl, girls) walked with them.

3. She wore a black (robe, robes).

4. There were two red (star, stars) on it.

5. It also had one orange (moon, moons).

6. The children walked up to a (house, houses).

7. Then, they knocked on a big (door, doors).

8. Will they ask for some (treat, treats)?

9. Then, the children saw two (cat, cats).

10. Two (dog, dogs) ran down the street.

11. An (owl, owls) hooted in the darkness.

12. Many (star, stars) were in the sky.

13. The wind blew through all the (tree, trees).

14. The children clapped their (hand, hands).

Name _____ Date _____

More Plural Nouns

> • Add **es** to nouns that end with **x**, **ss**, **ch**, or **sh** to make them name more than one.
> EXAMPLES:
> one fox, ten foxes
> one class, two classes
> one branch, five branches
> one bush, six bushes

 Rewrite these nouns to make them name more than one.

1. lunch _____

2. dress _____

3. glass _____

4. dish _____

5. box _____

6. watch _____

 Make the noun in ( ) mean more than one. Write the plural noun to complete the sentence.

7. Two _____ walk to the park.
(fox)

8. They sit on two _____.
(bench)

9. Their seats are only _____ apart.
(inch)

10. Then, they take out paints and _____.
(brush)

11. They bring towels to clean up the _____.
(mess)

12. They hope to paint the _____ near the park.
(church)

Language: Usage and Practice 2, SV 1419027794

Name _____ Date _____

One and More Than One

> • Add <u>s</u> to most nouns to make them name more than one.
>   EXAMPLE: one book, four book**s**

 Rewrite each noun to make it name more than one.

1. cap _____   **4.** tree _____

2. chair _____   **5.** flag _____

3. girl _____   **6.** boy _____

> • Add <u>es</u> to nouns that end with <u>x</u>, <u>ss</u>, <u>ch</u>, or <u>sh</u> to make them name more than one.
>   EXAMPLE: one lunch, five lunch**es**

 Rewrite each noun to make it name more than one.

7. ranch _____   **10.** dish _____

8. dress _____   **11.** box _____

9. glass _____   **12.** watch _____

 Write the word on the line that will complete each phrase. Add <u>s</u> or <u>es</u>.

13. two _____   **17.** six _____
　　　　　(pond)　　　　　　　　　　　　　　　　(wish)

14. many _____   **18.** five _____
　　　　　(pig)　　　　　　　　　　　　　　　　(bench)

15. three _____   **19.** four _____
　　　　　(brush)　　　　　　　　　　　　　　　(ax)

16. ten _____   **20.** a few _____
　　　　　(frog)　　　　　　　　　　　　　　　(ball)

Language: Usage and Practice 2, SV 1419027794

Irregular Plural Nouns

> • Some nouns change spelling to name more than one.
>   EXAMPLES:
>   man—men
>   woman—women
>   child—children
>   foot—feet
>   tooth—teeth

 Circle the correct noun in ( ) to complete each sentence.

1. One (woman, women) is working.

2. Many (men, man) are on horses.

3. A (child, children) is wading in the stream.

4. He has no shoes on his (feet, foot).

5. The cold water makes his (teeth, tooth) chatter.

 Make the noun in ( ) mean more than one. Write the plural noun to complete the sentence.

6. The _____ pet the dogs.   (child)

7. The little dog has big _____.   (foot)

8. The big dog has little _____.   (tooth)

9. Those _____ feed the dogs.   (man)

10. Those _____ walk the dogs.   (woman)

Name _____ Date _____

Action Words

- A verb is a word that shows action.
- Verbs tell what a person, place, or thing does.
  EXAMPLES: dogs **play**   We **eat**   Pat **reads**

 Draw a line from each noun to the correct verb, or action word. The first one has been done for you.

Nouns	Verbs
1. The boy	hops.
2. The baby	sing.
3. The rabbit	bark.
4. The birds	cries.
5. The dogs	reads.

 Draw a line under the verb in each sentence. The first one has been done for you.

6. Eric runs by Mr. and Mrs. Wilson's house.

7. He kicks a football into the air.

8. The ball breaks the Wilsons' window.

9. Mrs. Wilson looks out the door.

10. Mr. Wilson shakes his head.

11. Eric runs inside his house.

12. Mother talks to Eric about the window.

13. Mother sends Eric to the Wilsons' house.

14. Eric talks to the Wilsons.

15. Eric pays for the window.

Language: Usage and Practice 2, SV 1419027794

Naming Word or Action Word?

 Draw a line under the two nouns, or naming words, in each sentence. The first one has been done for you.

1. Our <u>class</u> is in our <u>room</u>.

2. Our teacher reads us stories.

3. Some stories are about elephants.

4. Elephants are very big animals.

 Draw a line under the verb, or action word, in each sentence. The first one has been done for you.

5. An elephant <u>takes</u> a bath.

6. Zoo workers put water on the elephant.

7. They rub soap all over the elephant.

8. Workers wash behind the elephant's ears.

9. Workers pour more water on the elephant.

 Read the sentences. Write <u>noun</u> or <u>verb</u> for each underlined word.

10. The wind <u>blows</u> hard today. _____

11. <u>Cristi</u> and Carl fly their kites. _____

12. The <u>kites</u> go up high. _____

13. They <u>climb</u> into the sky. _____

14. Carl's kite <u>string</u> breaks. _____

15. His kite <u>flies</u> away. _____

16. Cristi shares her kite with <u>Carl</u>. _____

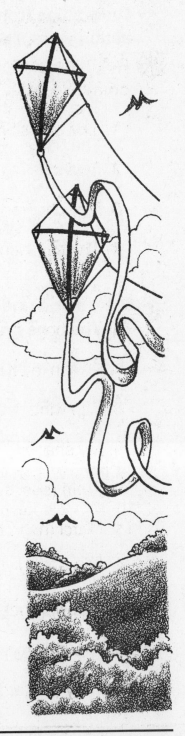

Unit 4: Grammar and Usage
Language: Usage and Practice 2, SV 1419027794

Name _____ Date _____

Singular Verbs

- Add <u>s</u> to an action verb that tells about one person or thing.

    EXAMPLES:

    The boy walk**s** quickly.

    He see**s** his friends.

 Read the sentences. Circle the correct verb in ( ) to complete each sentence.

1. The cat (skip, skips) down the steps.

2. Two cats (play, plays) on the stairs.

3. The children (hug, hugs) the cat.

4. The cat (purr, purrs) happily.

5. A puppy (bark, barks) at the cat.

6. The boys (hide, hides) from the girls.

7. A monkey (wave, waves) to them.

8. The wind (blow, blows) the trees.

9. My shadow (follow, follows) me.

10. A girl (see, sees) a shadow.

11. Marci (hear, hears) the tree speak.

12. The branches (move, moves) in the wind.

13. An owl (hoot, hoots) in the tree.

14. The children (take, takes) their treats home.

15. They (eat, eats) some fruit.

Helping Verbs

> • A helping verb works with the main verb to show action.
> • Use <u>has</u>, <u>have</u>, and <u>had</u> with other verbs to show action
> that happened in the past.
>   EXAMPLES:
>   Chen **has** worked hard.
>   Brit and Katie **have** helped.
>   They **had** stopped earlier for a snack.

Circle the helping verb in each sentence.

1. Now we have arrived at the camp.

2. Jason and Luis have unloaded the car.

3. Mr. Garcia had shopped for food the day before.

4. Jacob has gathered firewood.

5. Something strange has happened.

6. A spaceship has landed nearby!

Circle the correct helping verb in ( ) to complete each sentence.

7. We (has, have) built a new playground.

8. Mom and Dad (had, has) sawed the boards before.

9. Donna (has, have) sanded the wood.

10. They (has, have) painted the fence.

11. My brother and I (has, have) raked the leaves.

12. But my mother (had, have) forgotten the leaf bags.

Name _____ Date _____

Verbs That Do Not Show Action

- Some verbs do not show action. They tell about being.
  EXAMPLES:
  A snake **is** a reptile.
  The snake **was** hungry.
- Use <u>am</u> or <u>was</u> with the word I.
  EXAMPLES:
  I **am** in the tree.
  I **was** under the tree.
- Use <u>is</u> or <u>was</u> with one person or thing.
- Use <u>are</u> or <u>were</u> with more than one person or thing.
  EXAMPLES:
  A lizard **is** in my garden.
  Two turtles **were** in a box.

 Circle the correct verb in ( ) to complete each sentence.

1. Reptiles (are, is) cold-blooded animals.

2. Some snakes (are, is) dangerous.

3. Many kinds of lizards (were, was) at the zoo.

4. A draco (is, am) a lizard.

5. Crocodiles (are, is) the largest reptiles.

6. The crocodiles (were, was) very noisy.

7. One lizard (is, are) in the box.

8. I (is, am) near the turtle's box.

9. The box (was, were) near the window.

10. The turtle (is, are) sleeping.

Language: Usage and Practice 2, SV 1419027794

Name _____ Date _____

Present-Time Verbs

- Present-time verbs tell about action that happens now.
  EXAMPLE: Max and Lisa **walk** to school.
- Add <u>s</u> to an action verb that tells about one person or thing.
  EXAMPLE: Lisa **walks** to school.

 Circle the correct verb in ( ) to complete each sentence.

1. Max (play, plays) baseball.

2. He (run, runs) fast.

3. The girls (dance, dances) to the music.

4. Some friends (wait, waits) for Max.

5. Lisa (leap, leaps) across the floor.

 Finish the story. Write action verbs. You may use words from the box.

sits	asks	walks
stands	takes	dances

Sam **(6)** _____ his sister to her dancing class.

He **(7)** _____ on a chair to watch. The teacher

(8) _____ him to join the class. First, he **(9)** _____

with a girl. Then, he **(10)** _____ by a wall. Last, he

(11) _____ home.

Language: Usage and Practice 2, SV 1419027794

Name _____ Date _____

Using Is or Are

- Use <u>is</u> and <u>are</u> to tell about something that is happening now.
- Use <u>is</u> to tell about one person, place, or thing.
  EXAMPLE: Judy **is** going.
- Use <u>are</u> to tell about more than one person, place, or thing.
  EXAMPLES: Lynne and Ed **are** skating.
  The cats **are** sleeping.
- Use <u>are</u> with the word <u>you</u>.
  EXAMPLES: You **are** lost.   **Are** you happy?

 Write <u>is</u> or <u>are</u> to complete each sentence.
The first one is done for you.

1. We ___are___ going to the park.

2. Ali _____ going, too.

3. Kate and her sister _____ running.

4. Kate _____ the faster runner.

5. Where _____ the twins?

6. They _____ climbing a tree.

7. You _____ going to climb, too.

8. The children _____ having fun.

One duck **is** here.

Many ducks **are** here.

 Write one sentence about a park using <u>is</u>.
Write one sentence about a park using <u>are</u>.

9. (is) _____

10. (are) _____

Unit 4: Grammar and Usage
Language: Usage and Practice 2, SV 1419027794

Name _____ Date _____

Using <u>Do</u> or <u>Does</u>

- Use <u>does</u> to tell about one person, place, or thing.
  EXAMPLE: William **does** the work.
- Use <u>do</u> to tell about more than one person, place, or thing.
  EXAMPLE: They **do** the work.
- Also use <u>do</u> with the words <u>you</u> and <u>I</u>.
  EXAMPLES: I **do** the work.
  You **do** the work.

 Write <u>do</u> or <u>does</u> to complete each sentence.

1. We _____ a lot of work in the house.

2. My dad _____ all the dishes.

3. My mom _____ the windows.

4. My sister _____ the sweeping.

5. My grandma _____ the sewing.

6. I _____ the floor.

7. My little brother _____ the dusting.

8. I _____ not cook yet.

9. My little sister _____ put away toys.

10. We all _____ some work in our house.

 Write one sentence about yourself using <u>do</u>.
Write one sentence about a friend using <u>does</u>.

11. (do) _____

12. (does) _____

Language: Usage and Practice 2, SV 1419027794

Name _____ Date _____

Past-Time Verbs

- Verbs can tell about actions in the past.
- Form the past tense of most verbs by adding ed.
  EXAMPLE: Jo **planted** vegetables yesterday.

 Make each sentence tell about the past. Circle the correct verb in ( ) to complete each sentence.

1. Jeff (plays, played) with his sister.

2. The family (visited, visits) Grandmother often.

3. Mary (looks, looked) out the window.

4. Then, she (jumped, jumps) up and down.

5. Grandmother (leans, leaned) back on the pillow.

6. Mary (helps, helped) Grandmother.

7. Grandmother (laughs, laughed) at the baby chicks.

 Change each sentence. Make the verb tell about the past. Write the new sentence.

8. The girls play in the park.

_____

9. They climb over rocks.

_____

10. Their fathers call to them.

_____

Unit 4: Grammar and Usage
Language: Usage and Practice 2, SV 1419027794

Adding ed or ing to Verbs

- To show that something happened in the past, add ed to most verbs.
    EXAMPLE: Don **visited** Liz yesterday.
- To show that something is happening now, you can add ing to most verbs.
    EXAMPLE: Sue is **visiting** Liz now.

※ **Draw a line under the correct verb.**

1. Terry and Joe (played, playing) basketball last week.

2. Amy (called, calling) to them.

3. She (wanted, wanting) to play, too.

4. The boys (laughed, laughing) at her.

5. But Amy (jumped, jumping) for the ball.

6. She (played, playing) well.

7. Terry and Joe are not (laughed, laughing) anymore.

8. Now Amy is (played, playing) on their team.

9. Everyone is (talked, talking) about all the games they've won.

※ **Add ed or ing to each verb. Then, rewrite each sentence.**

10. Carmen is finish _____ her work now.

    _____

11. Carmen help _____ Grandma cook yesterday.

    _____

12. Grandma is cook _____ some soup today.

    _____

Irregular Verbs

- Some action verbs do not add <u>ed</u> to tell about the past.

Present	Past
go, goes	went
come, comes	came
run, runs	ran

EXAMPLES:

The boys **went** to sleep.

A dog **came** to a farm.

The raccoons **ran** into the woods.

 Circle the correct verb in ( ) to complete each sentence.

1. Three robbers (ran, runs) out the door.

2. They (comes, came) back.

3. Four animals (goes, went) by the house.

4. The rooster and the dog (go, goes) into the kitchen.

5. The friends (run, runs) down the road.

6. A cat (goes, go) very fast.

 Circle the verb in each sentence. Then, write each verb in the past tense.

7. The man goes to the mill. _____

8. A donkey comes to town. _____

9. The animals come to a big house. _____

10. They run to the window. _____

Language: Usage and Practice 2, SV 1419027794

Name _____ Date _____

Using <u>Was</u> or <u>Were</u>

- Use <u>was</u> and <u>were</u> to tell about something that happened in the past.
- Use <u>was</u> to tell about one person, place, or thing.
    EXAMPLE: My bat **was** on the step.
- Use <u>were</u> to tell about more than one person, place, or thing.
    EXAMPLES: Ten people **were** there.
              The books **were** lost.
- Use <u>were</u> with the word you.
    EXAMPLES: You **were** late. **Were** you home?

Write <u>was</u> or <u>were</u> to complete each sentence.

1. The children _____ indoors while it rained.

2. José _____ reading a book.

3. Scott and Jay _____ playing checkers.

4. Ann, Roy, and Jami _____ playing cards.

5. Sara and Bill _____ talking.

6. Nicky _____ beating a drum.

7. I _____ drawing pictures.

8. You _____ dancing.

 Write one sentence about a rainy day using <u>was</u>.
Write one sentence about a rainy day using <u>were</u>.

9. (was) _____

10. (were) _____

Language: Usage and Practice 2, SV 1419027794

Using See, Sees, or Saw

- Use see or sees to tell what is happening now.
  EXAMPLES: One boy **sees** a dog. Two boys **see** a dog.
- Use see with the words you and I.
  EXAMPLES: I **see** a dog. Do you **see** a dog?
- Use saw to tell what happened in the past.
  EXAMPLE: Justin **saw** Natalie last week.

Write see, sees, or saw to complete each sentence.

1. Today Mike _____ his friend Leena.

2. He _____ her last Monday.

3. Leena _____ Mike paint now.

4. My dad _____ Mike paint now, too.

5. Mike _____ a beautiful sky last night.

6. He _____ pink in the sky on Sunday.

7. Grandpa and I _____ some trains now.

8. We _____ many trains on my last birthday.

9. We _____ old and new trains last winter.

10. Today I can _____ the train show.

**Write see, sees, or saw to complete each sentence.
Then rewrite each sentence.**

11. Last week we _____ Lee.

_____

12. Lee _____ my painting now.

_____

Unit 4: Grammar and Usage
Language: Usage and Practice 2, SV 1419027794

Name _____ Date _____

Using <u>Run</u>, <u>Runs</u>, or <u>Ran</u>

- Use <u>run</u> or <u>runs</u> to tell what is happening now.
  EXAMPLES: One horse **runs**. Two horses **run**.
- Use <u>run</u> with the words <u>you</u> and <u>I</u>.
  EXAMPLES: I **run** in the park. Do you **run**?
- Use <u>ran</u> to tell what happened in the past.
  EXAMPLE: Yesterday we **ran** to the park.

 **Write <u>run</u>, <u>runs</u>, or <u>ran</u> to complete each sentence.
Then rewrite each sentence.**

1. Horses _____ wild long ago.

   _____

2. A horse can _____ ten miles every day.

   _____

3. Can you _____ as fast as a horse?

   _____

4. Mandy _____ in a race last week.

   _____

5. Jeff _____ home from school now.

   _____

6. Now Mandy _____ after Jeff.

   _____

7. How far can you _____?

   _____

Language: Usage and Practice 2, SV 1419027794

Using <u>Give</u>, <u>Gives</u>, or <u>Gave</u>

- Use <u>give</u> or <u>gives</u> to tell what is happening now.
  EXAMPLES: One student **gives** a gift. Two students **give** a gift.
- Use <u>give</u> with the words <u>you</u> and <u>I</u>.
  EXAMPLES: I **give** a gift. Do you **give** one?
- Use <u>gave</u> to tell what happened in the past.
  EXAMPLE: Jeff **gave** me a present yesterday.

✳ **Write give, gives, or gave to complete each sentence.**

1. Can you _____ the animals some food?

2. Sandi _____ them water yesterday.

3. Juan _____ the chickens corn now.

4. Chickens _____ us eggs to eat yesterday.

5. We _____ the kittens some milk last night.

6. Who _____ hay to the cow then?

7. Our cow _____ us milk yesterday.

8. I _____ food to the pigs last Monday.

9. Maria _____ food to the sheep now.

✳ **Write three sentences about gifts using give, gives, and gave.**

10. (give) _____

11. (gives) _____

12. (gave) _____

Using <u>Has</u>, <u>Have</u>, or <u>Had</u>

- Use **has** to tell about one person, place, or thing.
  - EXAMPLE: Jesse **has** a bird.
- Use <u>have</u> to tell about more than one person, place, or thing.
  - EXAMPLE: Cars **have** tires.
- Use <u>have</u> with the words <u>you</u> and <u>I</u>.
  - EXAMPLES: You **have** new shoes. I **have** fun.
- Use <u>had</u> to tell about the past.
  - EXAMPLES: My dogs **had** fleas.
  - Bill **had** a cat last year.

✳ Write <u>has</u>, <u>have</u>, or <u>had</u> to complete each sentence.

1. My brother _____ a pet fish last year.

2. Now Zack _____ a pet mouse.

3. The pets _____ good homes now.

4. I _____ a football now.

5. Now Jordan _____ a pair of roller skates, too.

6. Yesterday Dawn _____ a full balloon.

7. Now the balloon _____ a hole in it.

8. She _____ the money to buy another balloon today.

9. You _____ many friends now.

10. Your friends _____ fun together last Saturday.

11. Last week I _____ supper with Eric.

12. Now he _____ supper with me.

Name _____ Date _____

Pronouns

> * A **pronoun** is a word that takes the place of a noun.
> * Some pronouns are <u>he</u>, <u>she</u>, <u>it</u>, <u>we</u>, <u>you</u>, <u>they</u>, and <u>I</u>.
>   EXAMPLE: **Bill** plays with Jim. **He** plays with Jim.

 Rewrite each sentence. Choose a pronoun from the box to take the place of the words that are underlined. The first is done for you.

He She It We They

1. <u>Alicia</u> got a gift.

    She got a gift. _____

2. <u>The gift</u> was for her birthday.

_____

3. <u>Jack</u> brought the gift.

_____

4. <u>Kim and Tim</u> found a box.

_____

5. <u>Ella and I</u> are going to the party.

_____

6. <u>Rosa and Luis</u> will wear hats.

_____

7. <u>Suzi</u> likes punch.

_____

8. <u>The party</u> will end soon.

_____

Language: Usage and Practice 2, SV 1419027794

Name _____ Date _____

Using I or Me

Use I in the naming part of the sentence.
EXAMPLES: **I** went to the movie.
Dad and **I** played cards.
Use me after a verb, or action word.
EXAMPLES: Mom gave **me** the ball.
Mrs. Ford helped Kathy and **me**.

 Circle I or me to complete each sentence.

1. (I, Me) wanted a job.

2. David and (I, me) tried to make money.

3. Mr. Garza gave David and (I, me) a job.

4. Mr. Garza told (I, me) to cut his grass.

5. David and (I, me) made four dollars each.

6. (I, Me) will buy a treat for us.

 Write I or me to complete each sentence.

7. _____ went on a trip.

8. Dad gave _____ a new fishing pole.

9. Ben and _____ went to the lake.

10. _____ had a good time fishing.

11. Mom and _____ went on a hike.

12. My sister read Ben and _____ a story.

13. Uncle Warren and _____ sang songs.

14. _____ was tired when we got home.

Unit 4: Grammar and Usage
Language: Usage and Practice 2, SV 1419027794

Using A or An

> • Use **an** before words that begin with a vowel sound.
> • The vowels are a, e, i, o, and u.
>   EXAMPLES: **an** apple, **an** egg
> • Use **a** before words that begin with a consonant sound.
>   EXAMPLES: **a** car, **a** skate

a	**an**
a ball	an apple
a dog	an egg
a skate	an elephant

Write a or an.

1. _____ arm
2. _____ dog
3. _____ hat
4. _____ ant
5. _____ cat
6. _____ elf

7. _____ ear
8. _____ office
9. _____ fire
10. _____ cow
11. _____ uncle
12. _____ tree

13. _____ inch
14. _____ ax
15. _____ top
16. _____ boat
17. _____ duck
18. _____ oven

Write a or an to complete each sentence.

19. Linda has two balls and _____ bat.

20. Victor has _____ old tent.

Name _____   Date _____

Adjectives

- An **adjective** is a word that describes a noun.
    EXAMPLE: The **old** woman walked home.
- Describing words can tell about color or size.
    EXAMPLE: **Red** flowers grow in the **small** garden.
- Describing words can tell about shape.
    EXAMPLE: The house has a **square** window.
- Describing words can tell how something feels, tastes, sounds, or smells.
    EXAMPLE: The flowers have a **sweet** smell.

 Finish each sentence. Write describing words from the box.

round	tiny
long	pink
brown	juicy

1. The woman puts on a _____ bonnet.

2. She walks down a _____ road.

3. Some _____ squirrels run by.

4. A man gives her a _____ orange.

5. The orange is _____.

6. Do you see a _____ bone in the yard?

Language: Usage and Practice 2, SV 1419027794

Name _____   Date _____

Using Adjectives

- Adjectives are describing words. Describing words can tell about feelings.
  - EXAMPLES: The woman was **surprised**.
    She was **happy**.
- Describing words can also tell how many.
  - EXAMPLE: She picked **four** flowers.
- Some describing words that tell how many do not tell exact numbers.
  - EXAMPLES: There are **many** roses in the garden.
    Some grass grows here.

 Finish each sentence. Write describing words from the box.

| happy | hungry | three | one |
| some | tired | sleepy | many |

1. The woman was _____ from walking so far.

2. She was _____ to be home.

3. First, she put _____ flowers in a vase.

4. Next, she put _____ carrot in a pot.

5. She was _____ and wanted to eat.

6. Then, she ate _____ soup.

7. She also had _____ crackers.

8. Last, the woman was _____ and went to bed.

Language: Usage and Practice 2, SV 1419027794

Adjectives That Compare

- Add <u>er</u> to most describing words when they are used to compare two things.
  EXAMPLE: This tree is **taller** than that one.
- Add <u>est</u> to most describing words when they are used to compare more than two things.
  EXAMPLE: The sequoia tree is the **tallest** tree of all.

 Read the chart. Fill in the missing describing words.

1.	long	longer	longest
2.	bright		brightest
3.	tall	taller	
4.		faster	fastest

 Circle the correct describing word in ( ) to complete each sentence.

5. That tree trunk is (thick, thicker) than this one.

6. The giant sequoia is the (bigger, biggest) living thing of all.

7. The stump of a giant sequoia is (wider, widest) than my room.

8. These trees are the (older, oldest) of all.

98 ft.

Language: Usage and Practice 2, SV 1419027794

Using Words That Compare

- Add _er_ to most words to compare two people or two things.

  EXAMPLE: Matt is **fast**.

  Clare is **faster** than Matt.

- Add _est_ to most words to compare more than two people or two things.

  EXAMPLE: Lance is the **fastest** of the three children.

 Add _er_ or _est_ to complete each sentence. Then rewrite the sentences.

1. Dad is young _____ than Mom.

_____

2. Kim is the old _____ of four children.

_____

3. An ant is small _____ than a pig.

_____

4. That snake is the long _____ of the six at the zoo.

_____

5. The barn is tall _____ than the house.

_____

6. Alex is strong _____ than Michael.

_____

7. That blue chair is the soft _____ in the room.

_____

Unit 4 Test

Circle noun or verb to name the underlined word in each sentence.

1. The swimming <u>pool</u> opens today.   noun   verb

2. I <u>jump</u> in the deep water.   noun   verb

3. Kenny and I <u>race</u> across the pool.   noun   verb

4. The <u>water</u> feels cool.   noun   verb

5. Some of my <u>friends</u> are at the pool.   noun   verb

6. The pool <u>closes</u> soon.   noun   verb

Choose whether the underlined words are proper nouns. Circle yes or no.

7. Is <u>Lisa</u> going to the party?   yes   no

8. Our whole <u>team</u> is going to the party.   yes   no

9. The party will be at <u>Pizza Parade</u>.   yes   no

10. Pizza Parade is on <u>Coral Drive</u>.   yes   no

11. What <u>day</u> of the week is the party?   yes   no

12. The party is on <u>Saturday</u>.   yes   no

Darken the circle by the noun that means more than one.

13. Ⓐ bag   Ⓑ yard   Ⓒ boxes

14. Ⓐ band   Ⓑ car   Ⓒ men

15. Ⓐ field   Ⓑ lunches   Ⓒ dollar

16. Ⓐ fire   Ⓑ ovens   Ⓒ class

17. Ⓐ foxes   Ⓑ puddle   Ⓒ sky

18. Ⓐ glasses   Ⓑ pond   Ⓒ flag

Language: Usage and Practice 2, SV 1419027794

Name _____ Date _____

Darken the circle by the correct word that completes each sentence.

19. Where __ the ducks go?   Ⓐ does   Ⓑ do   Ⓒ fly

20. Do you wear __ watch?   Ⓐ a   Ⓑ an   Ⓒ two

21. The squirrel __ up into the tree.   Ⓐ ran   Ⓑ run   Ⓒ fast

22. The boy said __ would be back.   Ⓐ me   Ⓑ he   Ⓒ our

23. Our friends __ at school.   Ⓐ is   Ⓑ was   Ⓒ were

24. I was __ by the tree.   Ⓐ wait   Ⓑ waited   Ⓒ waiting

25. Dan and __ played catch.   Ⓐ me   Ⓑ I   Ⓒ him

26. Can Pete borrow __?   Ⓐ we   Ⓑ she   Ⓒ it

27. The band __ beautiful music.   Ⓐ play   Ⓑ played   Ⓒ playing

28. __ has a part in the play.   Ⓐ She   Ⓑ We   Ⓒ Me

29. Did you bring __ apple?   Ⓐ an   Ⓑ a   Ⓒ two

30. This orange is __ than that one.   Ⓐ sweet   Ⓑ sweeter   Ⓒ sweetest

31. You __ finished working.   Ⓐ is   Ⓑ are   Ⓒ was

32. I do not know who __ are.   Ⓐ I   Ⓑ he   Ⓒ they

33. I __ that dog last week.   Ⓐ sees   Ⓑ see   Ⓒ saw

34. Do __ need anything at the store?   Ⓐ me   Ⓑ we   Ⓒ us

35. They __ us now!   Ⓐ sees   Ⓑ see   Ⓒ saw

36. I hope that present is for __.   Ⓐ I   Ⓑ me   Ⓒ they

37. He __ you his chair.   Ⓐ giving   Ⓑ give   Ⓒ gave

38. They __ nice friends.   Ⓐ have   Ⓑ has   Ⓒ do

Unit 4 Test
Language: Usage and Practice 2, SV 1419027794

Name _____ Date _____

Writing Names of People

> • Each word of a person's name begins with a **capital letter**.
>   EXAMPLE: **M**ary **A**nn **M**iller

 Rewrite each name. Use capital letters where they are needed. The first one is done for you.

1. mark twain _Mark Twain_____

2. beverly cleary _____

3. diane dillon _____

4. lewis carroll _____

5. ezra jack keats _____

> • Each word of a family name begins with a **capital letter**.
>   EXAMPLE: Here come **Aunt Ann** and **Grandpa Bob**.

 Circle the letters that should be capital letters.

6. Today mother called grandma.

7. We will see grandma and grandpa at the party.

8. Will uncle carlos and aunt kathy be there, too?

 Rewrite each sentence. Use capital letters where they are needed.

9. Did dad help mom?

_____

10. grandma and I played ball.

_____

11. uncle frank is visiting us.

_____

Language: Usage and Practice 2, SV 1419027794

Name _____ Date _____

Initials

> • An **initial** stands for a person's name. It is a capital letter with a **period (.)** after it.
> EXAMPLE: Steven Bell Mathis = Steven **B.** Mathis or **S. B.** Mathis or **S. B. M.**

 Write the initials of each name. The first one is done for you.

1. Robert Lawson _R.L._

2. Carrie Anne Collier _____

3. Marcia Brown _____

4. Michael Bond _____

5. Carol Frank _____

6. Teresa Lynn Turner _____

7. Isaiah Bradley _____

8. Lou Ann Walker _____

 Rewrite each name. Use initials for the names that are underlined.

9. Joan Walsh Anglund _____

10. Lee Bennett Hopkins _____

11. Jane Yolen _____

12. Patricia Ann Rosen _____

 Rewrite each sentence. Be sure to write the initials correctly.

13. The box was for m s mills.

_____

14. d e ellis sent it to her.

_____

15. t j lee brought the box to the house.

_____

Language: Usage and Practice 2, SV 1419027794

Name _____ Date _____

Writing Titles of Respect

- Begin a title of respect with a capital letter.
- End <u>Mr.</u>, <u>Mrs.</u>, <u>Ms.</u>, and <u>Dr.</u> with a period. They are short forms, or **abbreviations**, of longer words.
  EXAMPLES: **Mr.** George Selden   **Dr.** Alice Dahl
- Do not end <u>Miss</u> with a period.

 Rewrite each name correctly. Be sure to use capital letters and periods where needed.

1. mrs ruth scott _____

2. mr kurt wiese _____

3. miss e garcia _____

4. dr seuss _____

5. ms carol baylor _____

6. mr and mrs h cox _____

7. miss k e jones _____

 Rewrite each sentence correctly.

8. mrs h stone is here to see dr brooks.

   _____

9. dr brooks and ms miller are not here.

   _____

10. miss ari and mr lee came together.

   _____

11. mr f green will go in first.

   _____

Unit 5: Capitalization and Punctuation
Language: Usage and Practice 2, SV 1419027794

Name _____ Date _____

Writing Names of Places

> • Names of streets, parks, lakes, rivers, and schools begin with a capital letter. They are proper nouns.
> EXAMPLES: **F**irst **S**treet
> **R**ed **R**iver
> **C**entral **P**ark
>

 Rewrite each sentence. Use capital letters where they are needed.

1. James lives on market street.

   _____

2. I think thomas park is in this town.

   _____

3. We went to mathis lake for a picnic.

   _____

4. Is seton school far away?

   _____

> • The abbreviations of the words <u>street</u>, <u>road</u>, and <u>drive</u> in a place name begin with a capital letter and end with a period.
> EXAMPLES: Street = St. Main **St.**
> Road = Rd. Dove **Rd.**   Drive = Dr. East **Dr.**

 Rewrite each place name. Use abbreviations. The first one is done for you.

5. webb street Webb St.   8. hill road _____

6. airport road _____   9. bell street _____

7. doe drive _____   10. oak drive _____

Language: Usage and Practice 2, SV 1419027794

Writing Names of Days

- Names of days of the week begin with a capital letter.
  EXAMPLES: **M**onday, **F**riday
- The abbreviations of days of the week begin with a capital letter. They end with a period.
  EXAMPLES: **S**un., **M**on., **T**ues., **W**ed., **T**hurs., **F**ri., **S**at.

Sunday	Monday	Tuesday	Wednesday	Thursday	Friday	Saturday
		1	2	3	4	5
6	7	8	9	10	11	12

 Write the name of a day to complete each sentence.

1. The first day of the week is _____.

2. The day that comes before Saturday is _____.

3. The day in the middle of the week is _____.

4. Today is _____.

5. I like _____ best.

 Write the correct full name of each day. Then write the correct abbreviation. Use capital letters where needed. The first one is done for you.

6. sunday   Sunday _____   Sun. _____

7. monday   _____   _____

8. tuesday   _____   _____

9. wednesday   _____   _____

10. thursday   _____   _____

11. friday   _____   _____

12. saturday   _____   _____

Unit 5: Capitalization and Punctuation
Language: Usage and Practice 2, SV 1419027794

Writing Names of Months

- Names of the months begin with a capital letter.
- The abbreviations of the months begin with a capital letter. They end with a period.
  EXAMPLES: **J**an., **F**eb., **M**ar., **D**ec.

✳ **Write the months of the year correctly.**

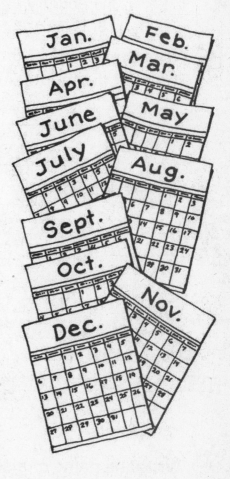

1. january _____

2. february _____

3. march _____

4. april _____

5. may _____

6. june _____

7. july _____

8. august _____

9. september _____

10. october _____

11. november _____

12. december _____

✳ **Write the abbreviations of the months correctly.**

13. jan _____   16. aug _____   19. oct _____

14. mar _____   17. sept _____   20. dec _____

15. nov _____   18. feb _____   21. apr _____

Language: Usage and Practice 2, SV 1419027794

Name _____ Date _____

Writing Names of Seasons

• Names of the four seasons do not begin with capital letters.
  EXAMPLES: **w**inter, **s**pring, **s**ummer, **f**all

winter	spring	summer	fall
December	March	June	September
January	April	July	October
February	May	August	November

✳ **Write the names of the four seasons on the top lines.**
Then list the months under the season.

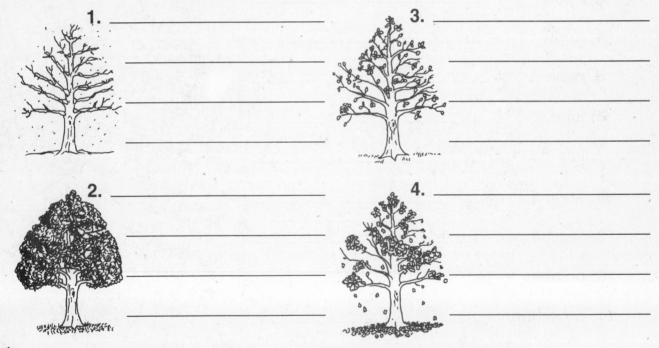

1. _____
   _____
   _____
   _____

3. _____
   _____
   _____
   _____

2. _____
   _____
   _____
   _____

4. _____
   _____
   _____
   _____

✳ **Write the name of a season to complete each sentence.**

5. In _____, we wear coats and gloves.

6. In _____, trees turn green, and flowers grow.

7. In _____, we swim outdoors.

8. In _____, tree leaves turn red and yellow.

Unit 5: Capitalization and Punctuation
Language: Usage and Practice 2, SV 1419027794

Writing Names of Holidays

> • Each word in the name of a holiday begins with a capital letter.   EXAMPLES: **V**alentine's **D**ay   **M**emorial **D**ay

 Write each holiday name correctly.

1. new year's day _____

2. mother's day _____

3. independence day _____

4. labor day _____

5. victoria day _____

6. thanksgiving day _____

 Rewrite each sentence correctly.

7. January 1 is new year's day.

_____

8. I like valentine's day.

_____

9. boxing day is a British holiday.

_____

10. father's day is in June.

_____

11. thanksgiving is on Thursday.

_____

12. We have a picnic on independence day.

_____

Writing Book Titles

- The first and last words in a book title begin with a capital letter.
- All other words begin with a capital letter except unimportant words.
- Some unimportant words are a, an, the, of, with, for, at, in, and on.
- Draw a line under the title of a book.

  EXAMPLES: The Snowy Day   Storm at Sea

 Write each book title correctly. Remember to underline book titles.

1. the doorbell rang

_____

2. best friends

_____

3. rabbits on roller skates

_____

4. the cat in the hat

_____

5. down on the sunny farm

_____

6. fifty saves his friend

_____

7. goodbye house

_____

8. the biggest bear

_____

Name _____ Date _____

Beginning Sentences

• Begin a sentence with a capital letter.
  EXAMPLE: Now Deena and Jet play together.

 Rewrite each sentence. Begin each sentence with a capital letter.

1. deena likes to play ball.

_____

2. her ball is red.

_____

3. jet wants to play.

_____

4. jet likes the ball.

_____

5. deena throws the ball.

_____

6. the ball goes far.

_____

7. jet runs to the ball.

_____

8. jet brings the ball back.

_____

9. deena hugs her dog.

_____

10. they have fun together.

_____

Unit 5: Capitalization and Punctuation
Language: Usage and Practice 2, SV 1419027794

Name _____   Date _____

Ending Sentences

> • Put a **period (.)** at the end of a statement, or telling sentence.   EXAMPLE: Carri is my friend**.**

 Rewrite each telling sentence. Use capital letters and periods.

1. Carri played on the baseball team

_____

2. she played hard

_____

3. she hit two home runs

_____

> • Put a **question mark (?)** at the end of a question, or asking sentence.   EXAMPLE: Is he your brother**?**

 Rewrite each asking sentence. Use capital letters and question marks.

4. what time is it

_____

5. is it time for lunch

_____

6. are you ready to eat

_____

7. do you like apples

_____

Name _____ Date _____

Periods

- Use a period (.) at the end of a statement.
  EXAMPLE: I like to read books
  about frogs.
- Put a period at the end of most titles of people.
  EXAMPLE: Mr. Hi Hopper wrote the book.
  These are titles of people.
  Mr. Mrs. Ms. Dr. Miss

 Correct each sentence. Add periods where they are needed.

1. Jake has a nice garden

2. The flowers are pretty

3. Jake gave Kara some seeds

4. Kara will plant them in the ground

5. Little green plants will grow

6. Ms Kara thought the seeds were afraid.

7. Mr Jake told Kara not to worry.

8. Mrs Jones told Kara to wait a few days.

9. Kara showed her garden to Dr Dewey.

10. Ms Rabbitt thinks Kara has a nice garden.

Unit 5: Capitalization and Punctuation
Language: Usage and Practice 2, SV 1419027794

Name _____ Date _____

Question Marks and Exclamation Points

- Use a **question mark (?)** at the end of a question.
  EXAMPLE: Who are you**?**
- Use an **exclamation point (!)** at the end of an exclamation. An exclamation shows strong feelings.
  EXAMPLE: Leave me alone**!**

 Finish the sentences correctly. Add question marks and exclamation points where they are needed.

1. Help

2. Did you hear something

3. My leg is broken

4. I heard it that time

5. Where did it come from

6. How should I know

7. We have to call for help

8. Do you have a phone

9. Help me, please

10. Who said that

Name _____ Date _____

Using Commas in Lists

> • A **comma (,)** may take the place of the word <u>and</u> if a sentence lists three or more things. Keep the last <u>and</u>.
>   EXAMPLE:
>   We took pencils and paper and crayons
>   and books to school.
>   We took pencils, paper, crayons, and books to school.

 Put commas where they are needed.

1. We go to school on Monday Tuesday Wednesday Thursday and Friday.

2. We draw sing and read on Monday.

3. Our class went to the post office the firehouse and the zoo.

4. We ran jumped laughed and ate at the zoo.

5. Elephants lions tigers and bears live at the zoo.

 Rewrite each sentence. Use commas, and leave out <u>and</u> where needed.

6. Pam and Kay and Pedro work hard.

_____

7. Pam sings and dances and acts in the play.

_____

8. Kay cleans and fixes and paints the stage.

_____

Unit 5: Capitalization and Punctuation
Language: Usage and Practice 2, SV 1419027794

Name _____ Date _____

Using Commas in Place Names

> • Names of cities and states begin with a capital letter.
> • Put a comma between the name of a city and its state.
>   EXAMPLES: **D**enver, **C**olorado **D**over, **D**elaware

 Write the names of the cities and states correctly. The first one is done for you.

1. akron ohio ___Akron, Ohio___

2. hilo hawaii _____

3. macon georgia _____

4. nome alaska _____

5. provo utah _____

 Rewrite each sentence. Use capital letters and commas where they are needed.

6. Barb lives in barnet vermont.

_____

7. Mr. Han went to houston texas.

_____

8. Did Bruce like bend oregon?

_____

9. Will Amy visit newark ohio?

_____

10. How far away is salem maine?

_____

Unit 5: Capitalization and Punctuation
Language: Usage and Practice 2, SV 1419027794

Using Commas in Dates

- Put a comma between the day of the month and the year.
  EXAMPLE: July 4, 1776

 Write each date correctly. Use capital letters, periods, and commas where they are needed.

1. dec 12 1998 _____

2. mar 27 2005 _____

3. sept 8 2001 _____

4. nov 1 1999 _____

5. jan 5 1955 _____

 Complete each sentence. Write the date correctly on the line.

6. Uncle Jim was born on _____.
　　　　　　　　　　　　　　　　(august 10 1967)

7. Chen's birthday is _____.
　　　　　　　　　　　　　　　(oct 17 1998)

8. Maria visited on _____.
　　　　　　　　　　　　　　(february 8 2003)

9. Dad's party was on _____.
　　　　　　　　　　　　　　　(july 29 2004)

10. Carrie started school on _____.
　　　　　　　　　　　　　　　　　(sept 3 2005)

11. Luis lost his first tooth on _____.
　　　　　　　　　　　　　　　　　(oct 20 2001)

12. I was born on _____.

Name _____ Date _____

Using Apostrophes in Contractions

> - A **contraction** is a word made by joining two words.
> - An **apostrophe (')** shows where a letter or letters are left out.   EXAMPLES: is not = isn't   can not = can't
>   do not = don't   are not = aren't

 Draw a line from the two words to the correct contraction. The first one is done for you.

1. were not   hasn't

2. was not   haven't

3. has not   wasn't

4. have not   weren't

5. did not   aren't

6. are not   didn't

 Write each contraction as two words.

7. isn't _____ _____   11. didn't _____ _____

8. don't _____ _____   12. hadn't _____ _____

9. wasn't _____ _____   13. doesn't _____ _____

10. can't _____ _____   14. aren't _____ _____

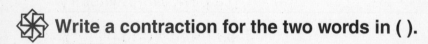 **Write a contraction for the two words in ( ).**

15. Today (is not) _____ a good day.

16. I (do not) _____ have my lunch.

17. I (did not) _____ finish my work.

18. My friends (were not) _____ on the bus.

Language: Usage and Practice 2, SV 1419027794

Name _____ Date _____

Unit 5 Test

Darken the circle by the sentence with the correct capital letters.

1. Ⓐ Mrs. Fuller drove to Byrne Park.

   Ⓑ mrs. fuller drove to Byrne Park.

   Ⓒ Mrs. Fuller drove to byrne park.

2. Ⓐ aunt julie visited elm school.

   Ⓑ Aunt Julie visited Elm School.

   Ⓒ aunt Julie visited elm school.

3. Ⓐ Dr. A. Hanson is here.

   Ⓑ Dr. a. hanson is here.

   Ⓒ dr. A. Hanson is here.

4. Ⓐ next monday is a holiday.

   Ⓑ Next Monday is a holiday.

   Ⓒ Next monday is a Holiday.

5. Ⓐ School Starts in the Fall.

   Ⓑ school starts in the fall.

   Ⓒ School starts in the fall.

6. Ⓐ I made a card for Father's Day.

   Ⓑ i made a card for father's day.

   Ⓒ I made a card for father's Day.

7. Ⓐ It snowed last january.

   Ⓑ It snowed last January.

   Ⓒ it snowed last January.

8. Ⓐ Turn left on Fifth street.

   Ⓑ Turn left on fifth street.

   Ⓒ Turn left on Fifth Street.

9. Ⓐ Carlos flew to Austin, Texas.

   Ⓑ Carlos flew to austin, texas.

   Ⓒ carlos flew to Austin, Texas.

10. Ⓐ J. I. Ross met R. P. Cain.

    Ⓑ j. i. Ross met r. p. Cain.

    Ⓒ J. I. ross met R. P cain.

Darken the circle by the book title with the correct capital letters.

11. Ⓐ Water life

    Ⓑ water life

    Ⓒ Water Life

12. Ⓐ Language Exercises

    Ⓑ language Exercises

    Ⓒ Language exercises

13. Ⓐ Voices from world history

    Ⓑ Voices from World History

    Ⓒ voices From world history

14. Ⓐ protecting wildlife

    Ⓑ Protecting Wildlife

    Ⓒ protecting Wildlife

Darken the circle by the correct short form for each word.

15. December   Ⓐ Decem.   Ⓑ Dec.   Ⓒ Dcbr.

16. cannot   Ⓐ cant'   Ⓑ can'ot   Ⓒ can't

17. Monday   Ⓐ Mond.   Ⓑ mo.   Ⓒ Mon.

18. Street   Ⓐ St.   Ⓑ Strt.   Ⓒ Str.

19. do not   Ⓐ don't   Ⓑ do'nt   Ⓒ d'ont

20. was not   Ⓐ wasn't   Ⓑ wasnt'   Ⓒ was'nt

21. have not   Ⓐ hav'nt   Ⓑ havnt'   Ⓒ haven't

22. Friday   Ⓐ Fr.   Ⓑ Fri.   Ⓒ fri

23. August   Ⓐ Agst.   Ⓑ Ag.   Ⓒ Aug.

24. Tuesday   Ⓐ Tue   Ⓑ Tues.   Ⓒ Tu.

25. are not   Ⓐ areno't   Ⓑ arn't   Ⓒ aren't

Darken the circle by the sentence with the correct periods, question marks, and commas.

26. Ⓐ Mr. J. Garcia was born on Oct 17 1975.

    Ⓑ Mr J Garcia was born on Oct. 17 1975.

    Ⓒ Mr. J. Garcia was born on Oct. 17, 1975.

27. Ⓐ Where was Dr. Blair on Apr. 12, 1999?

    Ⓑ Where was Dr. Blair on Apr. 12, 1999.

    Ⓒ Where was Dr Blair on Apr 12 1999?

28. Ⓐ Did you play on Dove St. last night.

    Ⓑ Did you play on Dove St last night?

    Ⓒ Did you play on Dove St. last night?

29. Ⓐ I will pack my clothes toys and books.

    Ⓑ I will pack my clothes, toys, and books.

    Ⓒ I will pack, my clothes, toys, and, books.

Name _____ Date _____

Writing Sentences

> • Remember that sentences have a naming part and an action part.   EXAMPLE: Sari won the race.

 Draw a line from a naming part to an action part to make sentences.

Naming Part	Action Part
1. Grandpa	baked.
2. Aunt Sue	sings.
3. My friend	skates.
4. Earl's dad	reads.
5. Kiko's mom	cooks.
6. Jon's sister	played.

 Write sentences with the naming parts and action parts you put together. Add some words of your own. The first one is done for you.

7. Grandpa reads the card. _____

8. _____

9. _____

10. _____

11. _____

12. _____

Write a sentence about a friend.

13. _____

_____

Unit 6: Composition
Language: Usage and Practice 2, SV 1419027794

Paragraphs

> • A **paragraph** is a group of sentences about one main idea.
> • The first line of a paragraph is **indented**. There is a space before the first word.
>   EXAMPLE:
>   Fluffy is my cat. She is four years old. She is black and white. She likes to play with yarn. She likes napping in the sunshine.

 Read each paragraph. Answer the questions.

   Charise is studying for her math test. The test is on Friday. She wants to get a good grade on the test. She knows that studying will help her do well on the test.

1. Who is this paragraph about? _____

2. Write the first sentence of the paragraph. _____

_____

   Today is my sister's birthday. She is five years old. She is having a party. Six of her friends are coming to the party. They will eat cake and play games.

3. What is this paragraph about? _____

_____

4. Write the first sentence of the paragraph. _____

_____

More About Paragraphs

- A paragraph is a group of sentences that tells about one main idea.
- The first line of a paragraph is indented. This means the first word is moved in a little from the left margin.
- The first sentence in a paragraph often tells the **main idea**.
- The other sentences tell about the main idea.

> EXAMPLE:
>
>   A safe home keeps people from getting hurt. Shoes or toys should not be left on the stairs. Matches, medicines, and cleaners should be locked safely away. Grown-ups should get things that are on high shelves for children. Then, children will not fall and get hurt.

How to Write a Paragraph:
1. Write a sentence that tells the main idea.
2. Indent the first line.
3. Write sentences that tell more about the main idea.

✳ **Write three sentences that tell about this main idea.**

There are many things you can do to be safe at school.

_____

_____

_____

_____

_____

_____

Language: Usage and Practice 2, SV 1419027794

Name _____ Date _____

Main Idea

> • The beginning sentence of a paragraph tells the main
>   idea. It tells what the paragraph is about.
>   EXAMPLE:
>   **I have nice neighbors.** Ms. Hill gives me flowers.
>   Mr. Stone always smiles and waves. Miss Higgins plays
>   ball with me.

 Read each paragraph. Write the sentence that tells the main idea.

Uncle Joe is a funny man. He tells jokes about elephants.
He does magic tricks that don't work. He makes funny faces
when he tells stories. He always makes me laugh.

1. _____

_____

Dad told us a funny story about his dog.
When Dad was a little boy, he had a dog
named Tiger. One day Dad forgot his lunch.
Dad said Tiger would bring it to school. A
friend thought it would be a real tiger.

2. _____

_____

Firefighters are brave people. They go into burning
buildings. They put out fires. They teach families how
to be safe in their homes.

3. _____

_____

Language: Usage and Practice 2, SV 1419027794

Supporting Details

> • The other sentences in a paragraph give **details** about the main idea in the beginning sentence.
> EXAMPLE:
> I have nice neighbors. **Ms. Hill gives me flowers. Mr. Stone always smiles and waves. Miss Higgins plays ball with me.**

✻ **Read each paragraph. Circle the beginning sentence. Underline the sentences that give details about the main idea.**

1. Uncle Joe is a funny man. He tells jokes about elephants. He does magic tricks that don't work. He makes funny faces when he tells stories. He always makes me laugh.

2. Dad told us a funny story about his dog. When Dad was a little boy, he had a dog named Tiger. One day Dad forgot his lunch. Dad said Tiger would bring it to school. A friend thought it would be a real tiger.

3. Firefighters are brave people. They go into burning buildings. They put out fires. They teach families how to be safe in their homes.

Name _____ Date _____

Order in Paragraphs

- The sentences in a paragraph tell things in the order in which they happened.
- Words like <u>first</u>, <u>second</u>, <u>third</u>, <u>next</u>, <u>then</u>, and <u>last</u> can help tell when things happened.

    EXAMPLE:

    Jane got ready for bed. **First**, she took a bath. **Next**, she brushed her teeth. **Then**, she put on her pajamas. **Last**, she read a story and got into bed.

 Write 1, 2, 3, or 4 to show what happened first, second, third, and last.

Eva planted flowers. First, she got a shovel. Next, she dug some holes in the garden. Then, she put the flowers into the holes. Last, she put the shovel back in its place.

_____ Then, she put the flowers into the holes.

_____ Next, she dug some holes in the garden.

_____ Last, she put the shovel back in its place.

_____ First, she got a shovel.

Dan and Larry washed the car. First, they got the car wet. Next, they put soap all over it. Then, they washed all the soap off. Last, they dried the car.

_____ They put soap all over the car.

_____ They washed all the soap off.

_____ Dan and Larry dried the car.

_____ The boys got the car wet.

Language: Usage and Practice 2, SV 1419027794

Name _____ Date _____

Parts of a Letter

- The **heading** of a letter tells where and when the letter was written.
- The **greeting** tells who will get the letter. The greeting begins with a capital letter and has a comma at the end. Each name in the greeting begins with a capital letter.
- The **body** tells what the letter is about.
- The **closing** says goodbye. There is a comma at the end. Only the first word of the closing begins with a capital letter.
- The **name** tells who wrote the letter.

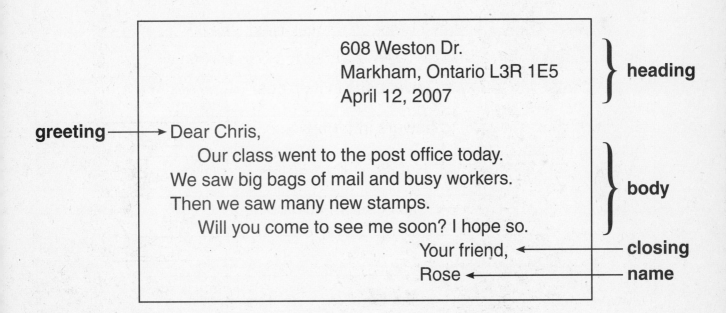

608 Weston Dr.
Markham, Ontario L3R 1E5
April 12, 2007   } **heading**

greeting ——→ Dear Chris,

   Our class went to the post office today.
We saw big bags of mail and busy workers.
Then we saw many new stamps.
   Will you come to see me soon? I hope so.   } **body**

      Your friend, ←—— **closing**
      Rose ←—— **name**

 Write the words about the letter to complete each sentence.

1. The letter is to _____.

2. The letter is from _____.

3. The letter writer lives at _____

_____.

Language: Usage and Practice 2, SV 1419027794

Name _____ Date _____

Writing a Friendly Letter

 Think of someone you want to write to. Use the organizer below to write your friendly letter.

heading _____

_____

_____

greeting _____

body _____

_____

_____

_____

_____

_____

_____

_____

_____

closing _____

name _____

Language: Usage and Practice 2, SV 1419027794

Envelopes

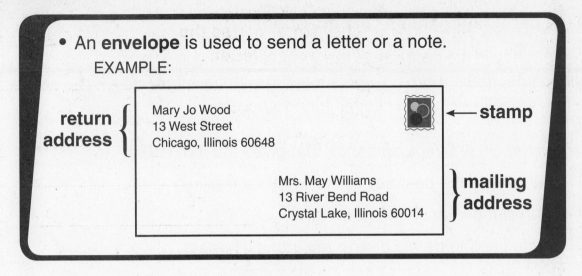

- An **envelope** is used to send a letter or a note.

EXAMPLE:

return address {
Mary Jo Wood
13 West Street
Chicago, Illinois 60648

← **stamp**

Mrs. May Williams
13 River Bend Road
Crystal Lake, Illinois 60014

} **mailing address**

How to Address an Envelope:

1. In the mailing address, tell who is receiving the letter.
2. In the return address, tell who is sending the letter.
3. Put a stamp on the envelope.

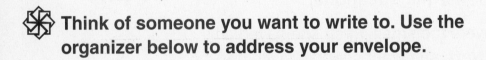 **Think of someone you want to write to. Use the organizer below to address your envelope.**

Language: Usage and Practice 2, SV 1419027794

Name _____ Date _____

Unit 6 Test

Read the paragraph. Answer the questions.

Saturday is the best day of the week for me. I can
sleep later in the morning. I go shopping with my family.
Sometimes I ride my bike to my friend's house.

1. Darken the circle by the sentence that gives the main idea.
   - Ⓐ Saturday is the best day of the week for me.
   - Ⓑ I can sleep later in the morning.
   - Ⓒ Sometimes I ride my bike to my friend's house.

2. Darken the circle by the sentence that gives a detail about the main idea.
   - Ⓐ Saturday is the best day of the week for me.
   - Ⓑ I can sleep later in the morning.
   - Ⓒ My brother likes Mondays.

Read the paragraph. Answer the questions.

Amy's old skates were too small. First, she saved all
her birthday money. Next, she went shopping with her
aunt. Then, she bought new skates that fit.

3. Darken the circle by what happened first.
   - Ⓐ Amy bought new skates that fit.
   - Ⓑ Amy went shopping with her aunt.
   - Ⓒ Amy saved all her birthday money.

4. Darken the circle by what happened last.
   - Ⓐ Amy's old skates were too small.
   - Ⓑ Amy bought new skates that fit.
   - Ⓒ Amy saved all her birthday money.

Name _____ Date _____

Look at the letter. Darken the circle by the correct name for each numbered part of the letter.

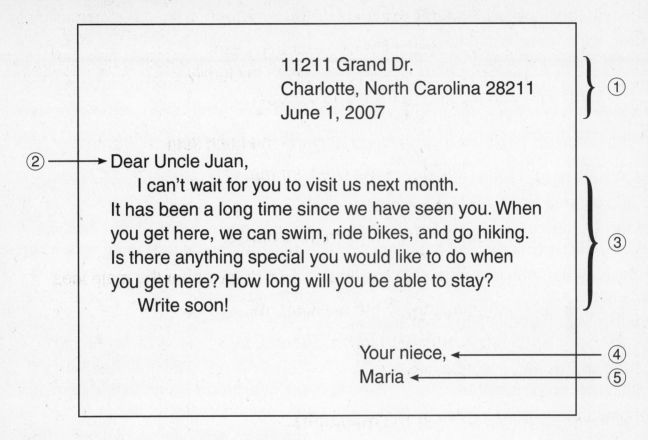

11211 Grand Dr.
Charlotte, North Carolina 28211
June 1, 2007 ⟩ ①

② ⟶ Dear Uncle Juan,
    I can't wait for you to visit us next month.
It has been a long time since we have seen you. When
you get here, we can swim, ride bikes, and go hiking.
Is there anything special you would like to do when
you get here? How long will you be able to stay?
    Write soon! ⟩ ③

       Your niece, ⟵ ④
       Maria ⟵ ⑤

5. What is part 1 of the letter called?

Ⓐ closing   Ⓑ heading   Ⓒ body

6. What is part 4 of the letter called?

Ⓐ heading   Ⓑ greeting   Ⓒ closing

7. What is part 5 of the letter called?

Ⓐ name   Ⓑ closing   Ⓒ greeting

8. What is part 3 of the letter called?

Ⓐ closing   Ⓑ heading   Ⓒ body

9. What is part 2 of the letter called?

Ⓐ body   Ⓑ greeting   Ⓒ name

Language: Usage and Practice 2, SV 1419027794

Language Terms

abbreviation   a short form of a word

action verb   a verb that tells an action that the subject is doing

adjective   a word that describes a noun

antonym   a word that has the opposite meaning of another word

apostrophe   a mark used to show where the missing letter or letters would be in a contraction

asking sentence   a group of words that asks a question; also called a question

body   the part of a letter that tells what the letter is about

closing   the part of a letter that says goodbye

compound word   a word made by putting two words together

contraction   a word formed by joining two other words

dictionary   a book of words in ABC order that shows how to spell words and tells what they mean

exclamation   a sentence that shows strong feelings

greeting   the part of a letter that tells who will get the letter

heading   the part of a letter that tells where and when the letter was written

helping verb   a verb that works with the main verb to show action

initial   a capital letter with a period after it that stands for a person's name

noun   a word that names a person, place, or thing

paragraph   a group of sentences about one main idea

plural noun   a noun that names more than one person, place, or thing

plural verb   a verb that tells about more than one person, place, or thing

predicate   the action part of a sentence

prefix   a group of letters added to the beginning of a word

pronoun   a word that takes the place of a noun

proper noun   a noun that names a special person, place, or thing and is capitalized

rhyming words   words that end with the same sound

sentence   a group of words that stands for a complete thought

singular noun   a noun that names one person, place, or thing

singular verb   a verb that tells about one person, place, or thing

subject   the naming part of a sentence

suffix   a group of letters added to the end of a word

synonym   a word that has the same or almost the same meaning as another word

table of contents   a list at the beginning of a book that shows the titles and page numbers of what is in the book

telling sentence   a group of words that tells something; also called a statement

verb   a word that shows action and tells what a person, place, or thing does

Language: Usage and Practice 2, SV 1419027794

Answer Key

Assessment
Pages 7–10
The following should be done:
1. Put an X on the apple.
2. Put an X to the right of the apple.
3. Put an X above the apple.
4. Draw a circle around the apple.
5. east
6. Shark Road
7. south
8. Dolphin Drive
9. two
10. pen
11. name
12. door
13. Carol, Thomas, Zena
14. carpet, door, window
15. dear
16. egg
17. dust
18. bill
19. box
20. to heat a liquid until bubbles form
21. knew, pan
22. angry, big
23. short, narrow
24. to
25. hear
26. there
The words in bold should be circled.
27. A, **Who**, took
28. X
29. T, I, bought
The words in bold should be circled.
30. **Mr. Donaldson**, grows
31. plants, **April**
32. were
33. We
34. a
The letters in bold should be circled, and punctuation marks should be added as shown.
35. **m**r. **t**. **r**. **w**iggins and **i** went to **d**aytona **b**each last **s**aturday, **s**unday, and **m**onday.
36. **r**honda went to the beach last **a**ugust.
37. **d**idn't she take her cat named **w**hiskers?
The sentence in bold should be circled.
38. **Julia wanted to bake her friend a cake for his birthday**. First, Julia read the recipe. Then she baked the cake. After the cake cooled, she put frosting on it.
39. 3, 2, 4, 1

Unit 1
Page 11
Read the following directions to students:
1. Draw a doorknob on the door.
2. Draw a chimney on the roof.
3. Draw smoke coming out of the chimney.
4. Draw a window to the right of the door.
5. Draw a tree beside the left side of the house.
6. Draw a car in the driveway.
Check to see that students have correctly followed your directions.

Page 12
Read the following directions to students:
1. Your mother wants you to do a few things when you get home from school. These are her directions: First, make your bed. Then, set the table. Finally, feed the cat.
2. Your friend invites you to come to his house. You have never been to his house before. Here are the directions he gives you: Go south on Red Road. Turn west on Green Street. Walk down two houses to 4202 Green Street.
3. Your teacher tells the class about a test. These are the directions: There will be a math test next Friday. It will be at 10:00. It will be on subtraction facts.
4. Your vet wants you to give your dog some medicine. Here are the directions: Give your dog one green pill in the morning. Give your dog a blue pill at noon. Give your dog another green pill in the evening.
Students should write the following key words:
1. 1) make your bed; 2) set the table; 3) feed the cat
2. 1) go south on Red Road; 2) turn west on Green Street; 3) walk down two houses to 4202
3. 1) math test next Friday; 2) 10:00; 3) on subtraction facts
4. 1) one green pill in the morning; 2) a blue pill at noon; 3) another green pill in the evening

Page 13
Check to see that students mark an X in the following places:
1. above
2. on
3. under
4. inside
5. beside, left
6. beside, right

Page 14
Check to see that students have colored the picture correctly.

Page 15
1. south
2. Fifth Avenue
3. east
4. Main Street
5. 5

Page 16
1. Robert
2. Sara
3. Robert
4. Sara
5. Robert
6. Sara
7. Sara
8. Robert
9. Sara
10. Robert

Page 17
Top: Students should cross out the following:
1. turtle
2. dog
3. elephant
4. frog
5. sister
6. popcorn
7. candle
8. mud
9. cry
10. blue
Bottom:
Colors: red, blue, yellow, green, orange, pink
Names: Josh, Mei, Roberto, Jennifer, Lupe, Vince
Actions: eat, sing, write, dance, skip, talk

Page 18
Check students' work for all letters from E to Z.
1. U
2. J
3. D

www.harcourtschoolsupply.com
© Harcourt Achieve Inc. All rights reserved.
Answer Key
Language: Usage and Practice 2, SV 1419027794

4. R
5. O
6. M
7. X
8. G
9. Z
10. Q
11. F
12. L
13. K
14. F
15. R
16. G
17. X
18. D
19. U
20. N
21. T
22. B
23. M
24. E
25. A
26. S
27. M
28. W
29. I
30. E
31. K
32. G
33. P
34. R
35. U
36. J

Page 19
1. 2, 1, 3; air, bat, cat
2. 3, 2, 1; rock, sea, top
3. 2, 3, 1; dog, egg, fish
4. 2, 3, 1; gate, hat, ice
5. 1, 3, 2; joke, king, lake
6. 2, 3, 1; mail, neck, owl
7. 3, 1, 2; us, very, well
8. 2, 3, 1; X-ray, yes, zoo
9. 3, 2, 1; nail, oak, pan
10. 2, 1, 3; air, bat, cat

Page 20
1. baby
2. bed
3. see/sit
4. fit/fun
5. race/run
6. fit/fun
7. race/run
8. see/sit

Page 21
1. middle
2. paw
3. open
4. noise
5. many
6. neighbor

7. to go back
8. never used before

Page 22
1. no
2. yes
3. no
4. yes
5. no
6. yes
7. yes
8. no
9. no
10. no

Page 23
Top: Students should circle the words
in bold.
1. **not warm**
2. a sickness of the nose and throat
1. **to fasten together with string**
2. a cloth worn around the neck
1. **moving water**
2. to move the hands back and forth
as a greeting
Bottom:
1. tie, 1
2. tie, 2
3. wave, 1
4. wave, 2
5. cold, 1
6. cold, 2

Page 24
1. Pets
2. 21
3. 7
4. 15
5. Fish
6. Rabbits
7. 7
8. 34
9. Dogs
10. Birds

Unit 1 TEST
Pages 25–26
1. C
2. A
3. A
4. C
5. B
6. C
7. B
8. C
9. A
10. B
11. A
12. C
13. B
14. A
15. C
16. C

17. C
18. A
19. C
20. B
21. B
22. C
23. A
24. C

Unit 2
Page 27
1. hop
2. ring
3. door
4. dish
5. ship
6. duck
7. coat
8. rug
9. tree
10. box
11. truck
12. wig

Page 28
1. road
2. home
3. sad
4. sick
5. gift
6. small
7. large
8. dog
9. yell
10. great
11. dad
12. sleep

Page 29
1. soft
2. long
3. dark
4. on
5. happy
6. low
7. dry
8. slow
9. bad
10. cold
11. go
12. hard
13. dirty
14. no

Page 30
1. hear
2. here
3. here
4. hear
5. here
6. here
7. their
8. their

Answer Key
Language: Usage and Practice 2, SV 1419027794

9. there
10. their
11. there

Page 31
1. their
2. They're
3. there
4. their
5. there
6. They're
7. They're
8. there
9. there
10. Their
11. there
12. They're

Page 32
1. write
2. right
3. right
4. write
5. right
6. write
7. write
8. right
9. right
10. write
11. right
12.–13. Sentences will vary.

Page 33
1. to
2. two
3. to
4. to
5. too
6. two
7. too
8. too
9. to
10. too
11. to
12. two
13. too
14. to

Page 34
1. a
2. b
3. a
4. a
5. a
6. b
7. b
8. a
9. a
10. a
11. b
12. a

Page 35
1. sunglasses
2. afternoon
3. playground
4. birthday
5. outside
6. scrapbook
7. sunglasses
8. afternoon
9. scrapbook
10. birthday
11. outside
12. playground

Page 36
1. unable; not able
2. reopened; opened again
3. unlucky; not lucky
4. unfair; not fair
5. unhappy; not happy
6. rewind; wind again
7. rewashed; washed again
8. uneven; not even
9. refilled; filled again
10. reknitted; knitted again

Page 37
1. careful; full of care
2. harmless; without harm
3. breakable; able to be broken
4. dreadful; full of dread
5. hopeful; full of hope
6. thankful; full of thanks

Unit 2 TEST

Pages 38–39
1. A
2. B
3. C
4. B
5. C
6. A
7. A
8. B
9. C
10. A
11. B
12. C
13. B
14. A
15. C
16. B
17. A
18. B
19. A
20. B

Unit 3: Sentences

Page 40
1. no
2. yes
3. no
4. yes
5. yes
6. yes
7. no
8. no
9. yes
10. yes
11. yes
12. no
13. yes
14. no
15. no
16. yes

Page 41
1. Mrs. Brown lives on my street.
2. Our building is made of wood.
3. Four families live in our building.
4. The students went on a picnic.
5. Jennifer was climbing the tree.
6. The sun shone all day.
7. Corn and beans grow on a farm.
8. The wagon has a broken wheel.
9. The mother goat fed the baby goat.
10. The boat sailed in strong winds.
11. The fisher caught seven fish.
12. Some of the fish were sold in the store.
13. Our team won ten games.
14. Our batters hit the ball a lot.
15. The ballpark was full of fans.
Sentences will vary. Check for completeness.

Page 42
1. My brother eats apples.
2. Bo drinks milk.
3. Kiyo likes peanut butter.
4. Justin wants bread.
5. Arturo plants corn.
6. Chang caught a fish.
7. Dad cooks breakfast.
8. Shawn shares his lunch.
9. Rosa grew the carrot.
10. Katie looks at the pie.

Page 43
The following sentences are telling sentences:
1, 2, 4, 5, 7, 8, 10, 12, 14, 15

Page 44
The following sentences are asking sentences:
1, 2, 4, 6, 7, 9, 10, 11, 13, 15

Page 45
1. statement
2. question
3. statement
4. question
5. statement
6. statement
7. question
8. exclamation
9. exclamation
10. statement

Page 46
Sentences will vary. Be sure each sentence is the specified kind.

Page 47
1. question
2. statement
3. question
4. statement
5. statement
6. question
7. statement
8. statement
9. question
10. question

Statements: I went to the toy store. I picked a game.
Questions: Are there any puzzles? Which toy do you want?

Page 48
Answers will vary.

Page 49
Students should circle the following parts of each sentence:
1. My family and I
2. Sandy Harper
3. Miss Jenkins
4. Mr. Olson
5. Levon
6. Mr. Byrne
7. Mrs. Osawa
8. Mr. and Mrs. Diaz
9. Jeanie
10. Mr. Wolf
11. Tom Taft
12. Mr. O'Dowd
13. Matt
14. Some children
15. Mrs. Clark
16. Carolyn and Alberto

Page 50
Students should circle the following parts of each sentence:
1. live on a busy street
2. found a bird
3. drives very slowly
4. walks his dog
5. throws to his dog
6. cuts his grass
7. picks up her children
8. shop for food
9. plays in the park
10. brings the mail
11. brings the paper
12. cooks dinner
13. paints the house
14. plant a garden
15. washes her windows
16. plant flower seeds

Page 51
1. Lions
2. Zebras
3. A pig
4. A cat
5. My dog
6. Fish
7. Birds
8. fly
9. buzz
10. barks
11. quack
12. hops
13. roar
14. moo
Sentences will vary.

Page 52
Answers will vary. Possible responses:
1. stroll
2. race
3. pedal
4. speed
5. zooms
6. jogs
7. skip
8. travels
9. sails
10. shouts

Page 53
Answers will vary. Be sure each new sentence contains describing words.

Page 54
1. The ant climbed down a blade of grass. He (or She) fell into the spring.
2. The bird pulled off a leaf. He (or She) let it fall into the water.
3. The hunter saw a lion. He (or She) spread a net.
4. The lion and I live in the woods. We are friends.

Page 55
1. Jake gave seeds to Kara and told her to plant them.
2. Kara planted the seeds and looked at the ground.
3. Kara sang songs and read stories to her seeds.
4. The rain fell on the seeds and helped them grow.

Page 56
1. The farmer and his family stood in the doorway.
2. The hunter and the bear stayed with the family.
3. The mice and the children ran out the door.
4. The hunter and the bear went home.

Unit 3 TEST
Pages 57–58
1. no
2. yes
3. no
4. yes
5. no
6. yes
7. B
8. C
9. A
10. B
11. telling
12. telling
13. asking
14. telling
15. asking
16. action part
17. naming part
18. action part
19. action part
20. naming part
21. action part
22. action part
23. naming part
24. Sentences will vary.
25. She packed a lunch for the picnic.
26. Ava and Alex went to the movie.
27. Chad mowed the lawn and raked the leaves.

Unit 4: Grammar and Usage
Page 59
1. apple
2. bird
3. boy
4. car
5. chair
6. desk
7. girl
8. grass
9. pen
10. rug
11. tree
12. truck
13. The girl eats an apple.; girl, apple
14. A bird flies to the tree.; bird, tree
15. A chair is by the desk.; chair, desk
16. A boy sits in the chair.; boy, chair
17. The girl plays with a truck.; girl, truck
18. The truck is on the rug.; truck, rug

Page 60
1. Bob's Bikes
2. Bridge Road
3. China
4. Elf Corn
5. Gabe
6. Linda

Language: Usage and Practice 2, SV 1419027794

7. New York City
8. Ohio
9. Pat Green
10. State Street
11. I bought apples at Hill's Store.; Hill's Store
12. The store is on Baker Street.; Baker Street
13. It is near Stone Library.; Stone Library
14. I gave an apple to Emily Fuller.; Emily Fuller

Page 61
1. boys
2. girl
3. robe
4. stars
5. moon
6. house
7. door
8. treats
9. cats
10. dogs
11. owl
12. stars
13. trees
14. hands

Page 62
1. lunches
2. dresses
3. glasses
4. dishes
5. boxes
6. watches
7. foxes
8. benches
9. inches
10. brushes
11. messes
12. churches

Page 63
1. caps
2. chairs
3. girls
4. trees
5. flags
6. boys
7. ranches
8. dresses
9. glasses
10. dishes
11. boxes
12. watches
13. ponds
14. pigs
15. brushes
16. frogs
17. wishes
18. benches
19. axes
20. balls

Page 64
1. woman
2. men
3. child
4. feet
5. teeth
6. children
7. feet
8. teeth
9. men
10. women

Page 65
1. The boy reads.
2. The baby cries.
3. The rabbit hops.
4. The birds sing.
5. The dogs bark.
6. runs
7. kicks
8. breaks
9. looks
10. shakes
11. runs
12. talks
13. sends
14. talks
15. pays

Page 66
1. class, room
2. teacher, stories
3. stories, elephants
4. Elephants, animals
5. takes
6. put
7. rub
8. wash
9. pour
10. verb
11. noun
12. noun
13. verb
14. noun
15. verb
16. noun

Page 67
1. skips
2. play
3. hug
4. purrs
5. barks
6. hide
7. waves
8. blows
9. follows
10. sees
11. hears
12. move
13. hoots
14. take
15. eat

Page 68
1. have
2. have
3. had
4. has
5. has
6. has
7. have
8. had
9. has
10. have
11. have
12. had

Page 69
1. are
2. are
3. were
4. is
5. are
6. were
7. is
8. am
9. was
10. is

Page 70
1. plays
2. runs
3. dance
4. wait
5. leaps
Paragraph (Answers may vary.): takes, sits, asks, dances, stands, walks

Page 71
1. are
2. is
3. are
4. is
5. are
6. are
7. are
8. are
9.–10. Sentences will vary.

Page 72
1. do
2. does
3. does
4. does
5. does
6. do
7. does
8. do
9. does
10. do
11.–12. Sentences will vary.

Page 73
1. played
2. visited
3. looked
4. jumped
5. leaned

Language: Usage and Practice 2, SV 1419027794

6. helped
7. laughed
8. The girls played in the park.
9. They climbed over rocks.
10. Their fathers called to them.

Page 74
1. played
2. called
3. wanted
4. laughed
5. jumped
6. played
7. laughing
8. playing
9. talking
10. Carmen is finishing her work now.
11. Carmen helped Grandma cook yesterday.
12. Grandma is cooking some soup today.

Page 75
1. ran
2. came
3. went
4. go
5. run
6. goes
7. goes, went
8. comes, came
9. come, came
10. run, ran

Page 76
1. were
2. was
3. were
4. were
5. were
6. was
7. was
8. were
9.–10. Sentences will vary.

Page 77
1. sees
2. saw
3. sees
4. sees
5. saw
6. saw
7. see
8. saw
9. saw
10. see
11. saw; Last week we saw Lee.
12. sees; Lee sees my painting now.

Page 78
1. ran; Horses ran wild long ago.
2. run; A horse can run ten miles every day.

3. run; Can you run as fast as a horse?
4. ran; Mandy ran in a race last week.
5. runs; Jeff runs home from school now.
6. runs; Now Mandy runs after Jeff.
7. run; How far can you run?

Page 79
1. give
2. gave
3. gives
4. gave
5. gave
6. gave
7. gave
8. gave
9. gives
10.–12. Sentences will vary.

Page 80
1. had
2. has
3. have
4. have
5. has
6. had
7. has
8. has
9. have
10. had
11. had
12. has

Page 81
1. She got a gift.
2. It was for her birthday.
3. He brought the gift.
4. They found a box.
5. We are going to the party.
6. They will wear hats.
7. She likes punch.
8. It will end soon.

Page 82
1. I
2. I
3. me
4. me
5. I
6. I
7. I
8. me
9. I
10. I
11. I
12. me
13. I
14. I

Page 83
1. an
2. a

3. a
4. an
5. a
6. an
7. an
8. an
9. a
10. a
11. an
12. a
13. an
14. an
15. a
16. a
17. a
18. an
19. a
20. an

Page 84
Answers may vary.
1. pink
2. long
3. brown
4. round
5. juicy
6. tiny

Page 85
Answers may vary.
1. tired
2. happy
3. many
4. one
5. hungry
6. some
7. three
8. sleepy

Page 86
2. brighter
3. tallest
4. fast
5. thicker
6. biggest
7. wider
8. oldest

Page 87
1. younger; Dad is younger than Mom.
2. oldest; Kim is the oldest of four children.
3. smaller; An ant is smaller than a pig.
4. longest; That snake is the longest of the six at the zoo.
5. taller; The barn is taller than the house.
6. stronger; Alex is stronger than Michael.
7. softest; That blue chair is the softest in the room.

Language: Usage and Practice 2, SV 1419027794

Unit 4 TEST
Pages 88–89
1. noun
2. verb
3. verb
4. noun
5. noun
6. verb
7. yes
8. no
9. yes
10. yes
11. no
12. yes
13. C
14. C
15. B
16. B
17. A
18. A
19. B
20. A
21. A
22. B
23. C
24. C
25. B
26. C
27. B
28. A
29. A
30. B
31. B
32. C
33. C
34. B
35. B
36. B
37. C
38. A

Unit 5: Capitalization and Punctuation
Page 90
1. Mark Twain
2. Beverly Cleary
3. Diane Dillon
4. Lewis Carroll
5. Ezra Jack Keats

Students should circle the first letter of the following:
6. mother, grandma
7. grandma, grandpa
8. uncle carlos, aunt kathy
9. Did Dad help Mom?
10. Grandma and I played ball.
11. Uncle Frank is visiting us.

Page 91
1. R.L.
2. C.A.C.
3. M.B.
4. M.B.
5. C.F.
6. T.L.T.
7. I.B.
8. L.A.W.
9. J. W. A.
10. L. B. Hopkins
11. J. Yolen
12. P.A.R.
13. The box was for M. S. Mills.
14. D. E. Ellis sent it to her.
15. T. J. Lee brought the box to the house.

Page 92
1. Mrs. Ruth Scott
2. Mr. Kurt Wiese
3. Miss E. Garcia
4. Dr. Seuss
5. Ms. Carol Baylor
6. Mr. and Mrs. H. Cox
7. Miss K. E. Jones
8. Mrs. H. Stone is here to see Dr. Brooks.
9. Dr. Brooks and Ms. Miller are not here.
10. Miss Ari and Mr. Lee came together.
11. Mr. F. Green will go in first.

Page 93
1. James lives on Market Street.
2. I think Thomas Park is in this town.
3. We went to Mathis Lake for a picnic.
4. Is Seton School far away?
5. Webb St.
6. Airport Rd.
7. Doe Dr.
8. Hill Rd.
9. Bell St.
10. Oak Dr.

Page 94
1. Sunday
2. Friday
3. Wednesday
4.–5. Answers will vary.
6. Sunday, Sun.
7. Monday, Mon.
8. Tuesday, Tues.
9. Wednesday, Wed.
10. Thursday, Thurs.
11. Friday, Fri.
12. Saturday, Sat.

Page 95
1. January
2. February
3. March
4. April
5. May
6. June
7. July
8. August
9. September
10. October
11. November
12. December
13. Jan.
14. Mar.
15. Nov.
16. Aug.
17. Sept.
18. Feb.
19. Oct.
20. Dec.
21. Apr.

Page 96
1. winter: December, January, February
2. summer: June, July, August
3. spring: March, April, May
4. fall: September, October, November
5. winter
6. spring
7. summer
8. fall

Page 97
1. New Year's Day
2. Mother's Day
3. Independence Day
4. Labor Day
5. Victoria Day
6. Thanksgiving Day
7. January 1 is New Year's Day.
8. I like Valentine's Day.
9. Boxing Day is a British holiday.
10. Father's Day is in June.
11. Thanksgiving is on Thursday.
12. We have a picnic on Independence Day.

Page 98
1. The Doorbell Rang
2. Best Friends
3. Rabbits on Roller Skates
4. The Cat in the Hat
5. Down on the Sunny Farm
6. Fifty Saves His Friend
7. Goodbye House
8. The Biggest Bear

Page 99
1. Deena likes to play ball.
2. Her ball is red.
3. Jet wants to play.
4. Jet likes the ball.
5. Deena throws the ball.
6. The ball goes far.
7. Jet runs to the ball.
8. Jet brings the ball back.

www.harcourtschoolsupply.com

127

Answer Key

Language: Usage and Practice 2, SV 1419027794

9. Deena hugs her dog.
10. They have fun together.

Page 100
1. Carri played on the baseball team.
2. She played hard.
3. She hit two home runs.
4. What time is it?
5. Is it time for lunch?
6. Are you ready to eat?
7. Do you like apples?

Page 101
1.–5. Each sentence should end with a period.
6. Ms.
7. Mr.
8. Mrs.
9. Dr.
10. Ms.

Page 102
1. !
2. ?
3. !
4. !
5. ?
6. ?
7. !
8. ?
9. !
10. ?

Page 103
1. We go to school on Monday, Tuesday, Wednesday, Thursday, and Friday.
2. We draw, sing, and read on Monday.
3. Our class went to the post office, the firehouse, and the zoo.
4. We ran, jumped, laughed, and ate at the zoo.
5. Elephants, lions, tigers, and bears live at the zoo.
6. Pam, Kay, and Pedro work hard.
7. Pam sings, dances, and acts in the play.
8. Kay cleans, fixes, and paints the stage.

Page 104
1. Akron, Ohio
2. Hilo, Hawaii
3. Macon, Georgia
4. Nome, Alaska
5. Provo, Utah
6. Barb lives in Barnet, Vermont.
7. Mr. Han went to Houston, Texas.
8. Did Bruce like Bend, Oregon?
9. Will Amy visit Newark, Ohio?
10. How far away is Salem, Maine?

Page 105
1. Dec. 12, 1998
2. Mar. 27, 2005
3. Sept. 8, 2001
4. Nov. 1, 1999
5. Jan. 5, 1955
6. Uncle Jim was born on August 10, 1967.
7. Chen's birthday is Oct. 17, 1998.
8. Maria visited on February 8, 2003.
9. Dad's party was on July 29, 2004.
10. Carrie started school on Sept. 3, 2005.
11. Luis lost his first tooth on Oct. 20, 2001.
12. Answers will vary.

Page 106
1. were not, weren't
2. was not, wasn't
3. has not, hasn't
4. have not, haven't
5. did not, didn't
6. are not, aren't
7. is not
8. do not
9. was not
10. can not
11. did not
12. had not
13. does not
14. are not
15. isn't
16. don't
17. didn't
18. weren't

Unit 5 TEST
Pages 107–108
1. A
2. B
3. A
4. B
5. C
6. A
7. B
8. C
9. A
10. A
11. C
12. A
13. B
14. B
15. B
16. C
17. C
18. A
19. A
20. A
21. C
22. B
23. C
24. B
25. C
26. C
27. A
28. C
29. B

Unit 6: Composition
Page 109
Sentences will vary.

Page 110
1. Charise
2. Charise is studying for her math test.
3. My sister's birthday
4. Today is my sister's birthday.

Page 111
Answers will vary. Sentences should be about school safety.

Page 112
1. Uncle Joe is a funny man.
2. Dad told us a funny story about his dog.
3. Firefighters are brave people.

Page 113
Students should circle the first sentence in each paragraph and underline all the other sentences.

Page 114
Top: 3, 2, 4, 1
Bottom: 2, 3, 4, 1

Page 115
1. Chris
2. Rose
3. 608 Weston Dr., Markham, Ontario L3R 1E5

Page 116
Letters will vary.

Page 117
Check that the envelope is filled in correctly.

Unit 6 TEST
Pages 118–119
1. A
2. B
3. C
4. B
5. B
6. C
7. A
8. C
9. B

Answer Key
Language: Usage and Practice 2, SV 1419027794